Framed Narratives

Theory and History of Literature
Edited by Wlad Godzich and Jochen Schulte-Sasse

Volume 1.   Tzvetan Todorov *Introduction to Poetics*

Volume 2.   Hans Robert Jauss *Toward an Aesthetic of Reception*

Volume 3.   Hans Robert Jauss
Aesthetic Experience and Literary Hermeneutics

Volume 4.   Peter Bürger *Theory of the Avant-Garde*

Volume 5.   Vladimir Propp *Theory and History of Folklore*

Volume 6.   Edited by Jonathan Arac, Wlad Godzich,
and Wallace Martin
The Yale Critics: Deconstruction in America

Volume 7.   Paul de Man *Blindness and Insight:
Essays in the Rhetoric of Contemporary Criticism*
2nd ed., rev.

Volume 8.   Mikhail Bakhtin *Problems of Dostoevsky's Poetics*

Volume 9.   Erich Auerbach
Scenes from the Drama of European Literature

Volume 10. Jean-François Lyotard
The Postmodern Condition: A Report on Knowledge

Volume 11. Edited by John Fekete *The Structural Allegory:
Reconstructive Encounters with the New French Thought*

Volume 12. Ross Chambers *Story and Situation: Narrative Seduction and
the Power of Fiction*

Volume 13. Tzvetan Todorov *Mikhail Bakhtin: The Dialogical Principle*

Volume 14. Georges Bataille *Visions of Excess: Selected Writings,
1927-1939*

Volume 15. Peter Szondi *On Textual Understanding and Other Essays*

Volume 16. Jacques Attali *Noise*

Volume 17. Michel de Certeau *Heterologies*

Volume 18. Thomas G. Pavel *The Poetics of Plot: The Case of English
Renaissance Drama*

Volume 19. Jay Caplan *Framed Narratives: Diderot's Genealogy
of the Beholder*

Framed Narratives

Diderot's Genealogy
of the Beholder

Jay Caplan

Afterword by Jochen Schulte-Sasse

Theory and History of Literature, Volume 19

 Manchester University Press

First published in the United Kingdom, 1986
by **Manchester University Press**
Oxford Road, Manchester M13 9PL

Page vi illustration: *Experiment with the Air-pump*
by Joseph Wright of Derby; reproduced with permission
of the Tate Gallery, London.

British Library Cataloguing in publication data *applied for*

ISBN 0–7190–1476–X
ISBN 0–7190–1477–8 *paperback*

Printed in Great Britain
at the Alden Press, Oxford

Contents

Framed Narratives

Introduction

Rien ne dissemble plus de lui que lui-même.
—*Rameau's Nephew*[1]

Like Jean-François Rameau, Diderot is a figure who has inspired a range of conflicting reactions in those who encounter him. The philosophe has been admired and despised, he has moved his readers and irritated them, and often at the same time. It has therefore seemed that the nature of those conflicts is the fundamental problem to be grasped in Diderot. From Hegel onward, Diderot's interpreters have tried to imagine a synthetic perspective from which the paradoxes could be resolved—to frame them, so to speak. In *Framed Narratives*, I have sought to pay more attention to this problem of framing *in* Diderot and *of* Diderot. I propose a model to describe how Diderot's texts devise a certain relationship with the reader, and I try to show how this relationship works at various levels of the text. In the concluding chapters, I extend this model to the realm of travel literature to speculate about the relationships between Diderot and "historical poetics."

Unfortunately, Diderot's work (like the figure of J. F. Rameau) makes a mockery of those who would fit it into a framework. Yet the philosophe's many interpreters can no more resist that temptation than he could overcome his desire to frame the overwhelming vastness and mobility of life. And so I shall begin by defining some of the terminology that I have used to "frame" Diderot: paradox, dialogue, and tableau.

* * *

Everyone knows that Diderot is a paradoxical writer whose works abound in logically irreconcilable, yet appealing positions. Like the Master Philosopher and the Nephew, Diderot's work does not easily fit into a single, coherent frame. Instead it continually shifts between mutually exclusive dialogic positions, neither of which provides an entirely satisfactory answer to the question at hand and yet neither of which can be disregarded, either. Some part of Diderot tends to be overlooked, either because his work resists synthesis or because the critic finds some aspect of the work uncongenial. Indeed, some would rather not touch his atheism and materialism, others his eroticism and body humor; and those who *do* find these aspects to their liking may be embarrassed· by his sentimentality. Yet these apparently heterogeneous elements are all parts, among others, of Diderot's text—which is not to say that this text is a "whole." Nonetheless, it is difficult not to suspect that the parts of Diderot that seem unrelated to each other, or with which one would rather not deal, can somehow be synthesized if approached from the proper perspective.

Many excellent studies have been devoted to dialogue in Diderot,[2] but I use the term to cover something different from what it usually means. In common usage and in literary criticism, *dialogue* usually refers to represented dialogue, such as that between the Master Philosopher and the Nephew, Jacques and his Master, and so on. Dialogue has meant symbolic interaction among *represented* interlocutors. In the present essay, I approach a series of texts, all of which contain represented dialogue, but do so from the standpoint of the dialogic relationship that they establish between the author and the reader— their implicit or explicit representations—a relationship that is mediated by the represented interlocutors. Technically speaking, I shall be concerned here more with utterance act (*énonciation*) than with utterance (*énoncé*).

At both levels of dialogue, Diderot is a paradoxical writer. The word "paradoxical" is not used here in its eighteenth-century sense of "contrary to received opinion," but in the more modern sense (which is also current in Diderot criticism) of "based on two contrary premises." Perhaps the best-known example of Diderotian paradox is the *Paradoxe sur le comédien*: namely, that what is proper to a great actor is that nothing is properly his.

Of course, this particular utterance also underlines the paradoxical character of every utterance. Indeed, since Benveniste and Lacan[3] it has become a commonplace that every utterance implies a splitting of the subject into two irreconcilable instances: the grammatical subject of the utterance (Benveniste's *sujet de l'énoncé*), and the instance ("person") responsible for the utterance (*sujet de l'énonciation*). Thus when the great actor performs, he brackets every dialogic gesture with implicit quotation marks. "It is never I who am speaking," he seems to say. The audience believes the great actor because it has momentarily forgotten the paradoxical character of the whole demonstration. For if the great actor never speaks for himself, who then is making the quotations?[4] On one level, the great actor implicitly claims that nothing could ever represent his own subjectivity for the simple reason that he has none; on a higher (logical) level, some kind of a subject is making precisely that representation. In this fashion, the subject of the utterance act frames the utterance.

In the case of the *Paradoxe sur le comédien*, we can say that "Diderot" makes the representation and that he addresses it to "the reader." "Diderot" is the subject of the utterance act, just as an interlocutor called *Le Premier* is the subject of the utterance. The relationship between the two has the form of a paradox. But who (as Lacoue-Labarthe has asked) is the subject of the paradox?[5] Clearly, it is not Diderot (or at least not the same "Diderot" who was responsible for the utterance act). Who or what is the subject of the paradox, and to what subject is it addressed? As I suggest throughout this book, this dialogic relationship, and the questions it raises, have implications that go beyond the work of Diderot. Of course, I also recognize that paradoxes underline the impossibility of establishing just this: what is "inside" an utterance and what is "outside." Nevertheless, I have tried to draw out some of these implications.

My interpretative model derives from what Diderot calls the *tableau*. Here again, the sense in which I use this term is not the familiar one. *Tableau* commonly refers to the theatrical device that Diderot invented as a means of replacing the *coup de théâtre* of French classical theater with something more appropriate to the conventions of middle-class life. In chapter 1, I show that the essentially imaginary character of the tableau makes it impossible to stage properly and that its real mode of existence is in the dialogic relationship between a certain kind of spectacular narration and its reader, or rather, its "beholder." The latter term, which I borrow from Michael Fried, serves to underline how Diderot's tableaux require their dialogic interlocutor to bear witness to a spectacle, to see it as much as read it. This borrowing from Fried's brilliant study[6] may seem inappropriate to some, since Fried went to great lengths to show how painting of Diderot's time aims to *exclude* the beholder from the painting. Yet I will show that, whatever the relationship in Diderot between the beholder and the painting, the beholder is required to participate in the tableau while also (paradoxically) being excluded from it.[7]

In any case, the conceptual frame of Diderot's "energetist materialism"[8] was itself paradoxical, or at least contradictory, because he believed that essentially life has no essence, that matter *is* movement. Already I find myself sounding like the Master Philosopher when he says of the Nephew: "Rien ne dissemble plus de lui que lui-même." I haven't translated this sentence yet because its precise meaning is uncertain: the verb *dissembler* apparently appears here for the first time in French. Barzun translated the sentence as "He has no greater opposite than himself."[9] Postponing my own interpretation until later on, I suggest that this description of the Nephew points to a kind of disjunction in his character. This disjunction can also be seen between the Nephew and his interlocutor, a feature that recurs throughout Diderot's texts. In *Rameau's Nephew*, as elsewhere in Diderot, the fundamental interpretative problem remains that of understanding the brilliant, and characteristically paradoxical, dialogic relations. It is a question of "framing" Diderot's dialogue.

Dialogue, in the sense in which I have been using it, is a notion that comes from M. M. Bakhtin. For Bakhtin, reality is human reality only when discourse addresses itself to other discourse. In his view, whenever we speak, write, or even think, there is a dialogic relationship at work that determines not only what we say (or write or think) but also who we are. According to Bakhtin, there are two major axes of dialogue. Every utterance addresses itself to an interlocutor and anticipates the interlocutor's reactions. Second, all utterances address themselves, explicitly or not, to everything that has previously been said about the same topic:[10]

> The dialogical orientation is obviously a characteristic phenomenon of all discourse. . . . Discourse comes upon the discourse of the other on all the roads that lead to its object, and it cannot but enter into intense and lively interaction with it. Only the mythical and totally alone Adam, approaching a virgin and still unspoken world with the very first discourse, could really avoid altogether this mutual orientation with respect to the discourse of the other, that occurs on the way to the object.[11]

It was not only for psychological reasons, or even for solely aesthetic ones, that Diderot cared so much about the dialogic relationship and for the opportunity it afforded for touching one's interlocutor as well as oneself. His affinity for dialogue had a philosophical basis as well. In fact, both his dialogism and his sentimentality are closely related to his brand of vitalist materialism.[12] Diderot had an affinity for the dialogic mode because it provided him with a way of both seeking after and revealing what he believed was the essential changeability of reality. Only in dialogue—in the shifting movements of conversation and dialogic confrontation—could he find a sense of his own identity, as well as approach the fleeting object of his thought.[13] To do serious thinking about the ever-changing nature of reality, he required a suitably mobile instrument of thought: dialogue. That instrument (or method) and its object were singularly well suited.

It is not the least of Diderot's paradoxes that for him the ultimate proof of the suitability of dialogue to thought would come with the defeat of its very instrumentality. As I will show, it was when dialogue finally touched him (and possibly his interlocutor), when it moved him to tears, so that he had lost all grasp over himself, his conceptual instrument, and his topic, it was then that he could sense that he had finally touched the mobile nature of reality. Here lies the paradox: to explore the essential changeability of reality, Diderot needed an equally changeable tool; on the other hand, the very mobility of reality would, almost by definition, defeat all attempts to discover it with conceptual tools. If dialogue is the only instrument suited to seek out and probe reality, it can only really "touch" its object when it has lost its instrumentality—when it is no longer quite a concept.

When truth appears, the philosophical subject finds himself overwhelmed by powerful feelings, and he momentarily loses his head, as it were. He "knows" (that is, he feels) that truth is nigh. What happens to the philosophe in these "sacred" moments[14] is that he senses the chasm between his own limits (his mortality) and a limitless, overwhelmingly moving reality. He recognizes the inability of thought to grasp reality, and thereby he momentarily gives himself the impression of having overcome his mortal limits. At such moments, the philosophe often cries.

Now myth represents the philosopher as a being detached from feelings, from his body, as well as from everything (received opinion or *doxa*, etc.) that might interfere with the exercise of his "higher" faculties. In modern times, we have the myth of Immanuel Kant as creature of Pure Reason, a being so (divinely) mechanical that the citizens of Königsberg could reputedly set their clocks by his comings and goings. Of course, whatever appeal it may hold even today, the myth of reality (and of the philosopher) as clocklike mechanism was no longer current in advanced scientific circles of Diderot's time, long before Kant walked the streets of Königsberg. This mechanical model had been replaced by the organic model of nature to which Diderot subscribed.[15] Nonetheless, even philosophers have tended to see themselves in terms of this idealist myth. In Aristotle's *Rhetoric*, for example, the appeal to pathos ranks lowest in the hierarchy of arguments.

For Diderot, not only does nature move but it is moving, as well. One aspect of Diderot's originality (and perhaps also a reason for his nearly total rejection by professional philosophers)[16] may lie in the subversive relationship that he establishes between philosophy and pathos. But what is moving about nature? The philosophe Diderot is moved by the workings of a "sacrificial" dialogic relationship, in part because of the sacrifices that virtue requires of him and his interlocutors. He writes (in the *Eloge de Richardson*) that "la vertu . . . est un sacrifice de soi."[17] ["Virtue . . . is a self-sacrifice."] Nature may indeed be movement, but it only becomes moving to Diderot when he thinks of (i.e., feels) the sacrifices of one's own changeability that virtue requires. In Diderot's eyes, Richardson does not use logic but makes one *feel* that "nous n'avons rien de mieux à faire pour être heureux que d'être vertueux."[18] ["We have nothing better to do in order to be happy than to be virtuous."] Virtue indeed does require (self) sacrifice, but that sacrifice makes one not only virtuous but happy, too, in the end. Thus will an apparent loss miraculously turn into a gain. We shall have occasion to see how Diderot transforms this Christian dialectic of sacrifice.

Granted that virtue requires sacrifice, but how marvelous it is to feel virtuous when one senses the effect that one's sacrifices will have on others (on one's readers):

Hommes, venez apprendre de [Richardson], à vous réconcilier avec les maux de la vie; venez, nous pleurerons ensemble sur les personnages malheureux de ses fictions, et nous dirons, "Si le sort nous accable, du moins les honnêtes gens pleureront sur nous."[19]

Oh men, come learn from Richardson to reconcile yourselves with the evils of life; come, we shall cry together over the unhappy characters of his fictions, and we shall say, "If fortune should overwhelm us, at least decent folk will cry over us."

The tear we shed today for Pamela or Clarissa, others will some day shed for us. When we are moved to identify with a fictional character and cry over her misfortunes, we address ourselves to the readers who repeat that sacrifice as they identify with us: as if we and our "readers" (and so on infinitely) were also characters in a novel (see chap. 3 and 4). At this point, what is the difference between fiction and reality?

Richardson's novels provide Diderot with a model for "real" experience,[20] a sacrificial model second only to the Gospels themselves:

Je comparais l'ouvrage de Richardson à un livre plus sacré encore, à un évangile apporté sur la terre pour séparer l'époux de l'épouse, le père du fils, la fille de la mère, le frère de la soeur . . .[21]

I compared Richardson's work to a book more sacred still, to a Gospel brought upon the earth in order to separate husband from wife, father from son, brother from sister.

Be they fictive or real, Diderot also imagines these sacrifices in terms of family relationships. Not only in his novels and plays but also (as we shall see) in philosophical texts, Diderot thought of the world in the familial terms so pathetically conveyed by the tableau. In Richardson's work and in the world, he remarks, "les hommes sont partagés en deux classes: ceux qui jouissent et ceux qui souffrent." ["Men are divided into two classes: those who bask in pleasure and those who suffer."] He adds, "C'est toujours à ceuxci [*i.e.* those who suffer] que je m'associe."[22] ["I always associate myself with the latter."] But the fact that Diderot "associates" himself with the suffering class of humanity obviously does not imply that the philosophe thinks of himself as one of them, nor does it mean that he belongs to the *jouisseurs*. Indeed, it will appear that no one, and least of all himself, fits neatly into either category of humanity because the entire human family has the capacity to experience *souffrance* and *jouissance* simultaneously. Such is the pleasure of what might be called "liberal" melancholy.[23]

C'est toujours à ceux-ci que je m'associe; et sans que je m'en apperçoive, le sentiment de la commisération s'exerce et se fortifie. Il m'a laissé *une mélancholi qui me plaît et qui dure.* [My emphasis]

I always associate myself with the latter; and without my noticing it, the feeling of commiseration is being practiced and strengthened. It has left me *a melancholy which pleases me and which lasts.*

The pre-Romantic pleasures of feeling melancholy and shedding an occasional tear were already becoming fashionable in Diderot's time. Reading novels had already become a favorite way of enjoying these pleasures. Moreover, like many of his contemporaries, Diderot also viewed the new genre of middle-class drama as a means of addressing the desire for this bittersweet pleasure. In the opening paragraph of his essay *De la poésie dramatique* (written in part to explain the failure of *Le Père de famille*), he imagines what would happen if a people accustomed only to light entertainment ("un genre de spectacle plaisant et gai") were offered the possibility of experiencing something pathetic and moving:

> Je me trompe fort, ou les hommes de bon sens, après en avoir conçu la possibilité, ne manquerait pas de dire: "A quoi bon ce genre? La vie ne nous apporte-t-elle pas assez de peines réelles, sans qu'on nous en fasse encore d'imaginaires? Pourquoi donner entrée à la tristesse jusque dans nos amusements?" Ils parleraient comme des gens étrangers au *doux plaisir de s'attendrir et de répandre des larmes.*[24] [My emphasis]

> Either I am badly mistaken, or men of good sense, after having imagined the possibility, would not fail to say: "What is the good of this genre? Does not life bring us enough real sorrows, without our being made to imagine new ones? Why should we let sorrow enter even into our amusements?" They would speak like people foreign to the *sweet pleasure of being moved and shedding tears.*

In fact, despite his awareness of cultural relativism, Diderot doesn't for a moment believe that such a people could exist. If a people were foreign to the pleasure of "being moved and shedding tears," for him it would simply not be human for it would (like the great actor of the *Paradox*) be lacking in the raw material of both human nature and life in general: *sensibilité.* The capacity to move and to be moved, *sensibilité,* is built into life. By nature, we are sensitive beings, that is, beings capable of moving others and of being moved by the representation of sufferings, fictional or real. If the human family is ultimately not divided into sufferers and *jouisseurs* (if it is really a family), it is because we have a sensitive nature; by virtue of our nature those differences can be overcome in fiction—or perhaps rather *as fiction*—and our suffering converted into "melancholy which pleases [us] and lasts."

Beyond the cultural differences that separate the human family, Diderot wants to appeal to a natural ground of *sensibilité.* Not just

because crying is universal, not just because "virtue" is a moral ob-
ligation, but because the tears that virtue moves one to shed provide a universal pleasure. Besides, when we cry for each other and
with each other—"Venez, nous pleurerons ensemble" ["Come, we
shall cry together] —we sense that the conflict between *ceux qui
souffrent* and *ceux qui jouissent* has been lifted. Our tears testify
that nowhere in the world can pleasure and pain be separated.
Somatic and semantic, biological and dialogical, the tear at once
expresses our universally sensitive nature and addresses itself to
our fellows. The pleasure of crying is a dialogic one.

In Diderot, the *jouissance* of dialogue cannot be separated from
a sense of imminent and irreparable loss, as if life were a novel and
each instant brought him closer to the final sentence. Consider
how Diderot recounts his first encounter with Richardson:

> Je me souviens encore de la première fois que les ouvrages
> de Richardson tombèrent entre mes mains: j'étais à la campagne.
> Combien cette lecture m'affecta délicieusement! A chaque
> instant, je voyais mon bonheur s'abréger d'une page. Bientôt
> j'éprouvai la même sensation qu'éprouveraient des hommes d'un
> commerce excellent qui auraient vécu ensemble pendant
> longtemps et qui seraient sur le point de se séparer. A la fin, il
> me sembla tout à coup que j'étais resté seul.[25]

> I still remember the first time Richardson's works fell into my
> hands: I was in the country. How deliciously I was affected
> by reading them! With each instant, I saw my happiness grow
> one page shorter. Soon I felt the same sensation that would be
> experienced by men of excellent company who had lived
> together for a long time, and were about to part. In the end, it
> suddenly felt as if I had been left alone.

From the moment he first "meets" Richardson, the pleasure of their
dialogue is heightened by an awareness that it must all come to an
end. "With each instant," the painful necessity of a final adieu makes
Diderot's pleasure more intense. Each page he turns makes his sense
of loss more acute, until finally his pleasure is transformed into
jouissance. Yet at this moment of total loss ("A la fin, il me sembla
. . . que j'étais resté seul"), Diderot has made such a pathetic sight
(or tableau) of himself that the reader-turned-beholder may be
tempted to repeat the process.

The reader of the *Eloge de Richardson* has his role to play, too.
The pleasure of "being moved and shedding tears" is always implicitly
shared, just as a tear appeals to interlocutors past, present, and future.

It is a pleasure experienced as dialogic, one that Diderot believes to have a universal social basis: as if everyone, regardless of class or gender, enjoyed a good cry. Diderot wants to write in genres that take that pleasure and make a spectacle of it. He wants to show that sentimental spectacles have universal appeal, that (unlike classical tragedy) they have nothing conventional about them. He sees sentimental spectacle as Aristotle did tragedy, as a natural genre.

For Diderot, the conventions of French classicism had been ignoring a crying social need, so to speak, a need that was no less real despite the disappointing failure of his *Père de famille*. The problem, Diderot insisted, lay not with the genre but with his own inadequacies as a dramatist.[26] Paradoxically, by arguing that crying is a universal, natural pleasure, Diderot lays the groundwork for a sociology of aesthetic pleasure.[27]

* * *

The method used here is neither sociological nor formalist, although I hope I have not slighted either the social context of these texts or their formal specificity. On the contrary, if language is dialogic (in the sense defined above), it must be understood as both form and content—although not necessarily as a synthesis of the two. The paradoxical nature of dialogue in Diderot generates figures of imperfect synthesis, of unmediated contradiction. Diderotian dialogue is not a simple, unmediated reflection of its social context, nor is it independent of that context. Diderot's texts address themselves to readers, but I have not taken these texts as fixed messages addressed by one preexisting subject (presumably Denis Diderot) to other preexisting subjects (his readers, as biological individuals). Rather, in keeping with both the theory and practice of Diderot, I have sought to describe dialogue as an open-ended interaction through which interlocutors and their language continually redefine and locate themselves.

The subjects (or readers) that dialogue seeks out and defines are not empirical, "skin-bound organisms" (Bateson)—such as "the real" Diderot or Sophie Volland—but they are not simply linguistic, and they are not immaterial, either. Rather they come into existence where bodies and language meet, in the realm of rhetoric.

The nature of my topic requires me to concern myself less with the positive-empirical conditions determined by literary sociology than with the social relations that Diderot's dialogue seeks to invent as it continually invents itself. From this perspective, it is less important to know the class position and gender of Diderot's actual reading public than to infer the rhetorical class and gender of the reader (or the author) that his dialogues engender.

Unlike the empirical position of the author and readers, their rhetorical positions may vary. As one reads, chemical processes within the body doubtless register these rhetorical shifts. Indeed, these positions (and the state of the reader's body) must change in specific ways if Diderot's text is to achieve its goals as dialogue. Those goals are to move, that is, to displace and to affect the reader; to move the reader (and the author, as he rereads himself) to tears. On the other hand, this kind of rhetoric is clearly the product of bourgeois society, and such rhetorical goals could hardly be set or achieved in a different society.

One last word about method. Although this essay contains readings of quite a diverse group of texts by Diderot—from the theory and practice of *le genre sérieux* to *Le Rêve de D'Alembert*, and from *La Religieuse* to the *Correspondence*—and although it draws its examples from an even wider range of Diderot's writings, it does not claim to be more than a partial reading of the philosophe's work. Furthermore, although I interpret certain of Diderot's works and provide a framework for reading others, my primary concern has been to connect these readings to general questions of what Bakhtin, with some hesitation, called "historical poetics."

Historical or sociological poetics was meant to be different from Aristotle's poetics, which describes the properties of certain types or genres of discourse as if these types were fixed and autonomous. For Aristotle, the relationship between a text and its audience is determined philosophically, by conditions independent of any particular time and place, rather than historically. On the other hand, Bakhtin's historical poetics conceives of discursive types or genres as dialogic, that is, as part of a larger semiotic context. We shall see that the dialogue between text and context—neither of which exists as an objective "fact"—is what makes both of them historical rather than natural. Historical or not, poetics is a discourse that uses empirical examples to construct types: the *Poetics* of Aristotle is first about tragedy and only secondarily about Sophocles' *Oedipus the King*. Here my topic is discourse that made people cry, rather than discourse that inspired "pity and fear." From readings of certain Diderot texts and from my own "supplement" on Bougainville, I have tried to make inferences about the common properties of pathetic discourse as it appeared in various Enlightenment genres.

In the following pages, I begin by describing a relatively simple level of dialogue in Diderot. I describe the spatial and temporal features of this figure, and certain social, political, and economic aspects of the world it implies. I then suggest relationships between this level of dialogue and the level of genre, specifically between the tableau and the new genres that Diderot advocated and practiced: namely, bourgeois drama and the novel (as distinguished from romance). At both of these levels, the dialogic relationship has a paradoxical character, which can be discerned in the emblematic figures of monsters and misfits. Finally, in the *Rêve de D'Alembert*, Diderot's paradoxical dialogue appears at a philosophical level. At this level, the paradoxical relationship that our analysis first described in the tableau seems to have acquired a kind of "epistemological" force. The identity of the philosopher (the subject) and of "nature" (his object) are most radically placed into question, and along with them the gender and genre of the "beholder" or reader.

The reader of this essay may detect a certain methodological inconsistency because the book appears to combine the perspective of "post-structuralist" formalism with that of literary sociology—all under the banner of Mikhail Bakhtin. For Bakhtin, the project of overcoming both the ahistorical character of formalism and the dogmatism of sociohistorical criticism was fraught with contradictions, some of which I shall address in the concluding chapter. Clearly, it is easier to invoke the "dialogic principle," to say that dialogue means "both form and content," than it is to practice that principle. If *Framed Narratives* lacks a unifying methodological framework, the reasons for this inconsistency lie not only in my personal limitations as a critic but also in the general context of contemporary criticism: and not only in that context, but also in the paradoxical nature of Diderot's writing.

I hope that these paradoxes will not have been entirely lost on me as I begin my own discourse "on" Diderot. In the famous last words of the Nephew, "He laughs best who laughs last."

Chapter One
The Aesthetics of Sacrifice

Qu'est-ce que la vertu? C'est . . . un sacrifice de soi-même.
—*Eloge de Richardson*[1]

In the second *Entretien sur le fils naturel*, Dorval relates a scene he has witnessed that he believes is made for theater:

Une paysanne du village que vous voyez entre ces deux montagnes . . . envoya son mari chez ses parents, qui demeurent dans un hameau voisin. Ce malheureux y fut tué par un de ses beaux-frères. Le lendemain, j'allai dans la maison où l'accident était arrivé. *J'y vis un tableau*, et j'y entendis un discours que je n'ai point oubliés. Le mort était étendu sur un lit. Ses jambes nues pendaient hors du lit. Sa femme écheveleé était à terre. Elle tenait les pieds de son mari; *et elle disait en fondant en larmes, et avec une action qui en arrachait à tout le monde*: "Hélas! quand je t'envoyai ici, je ne pensais pas que ces pieds te menaient à la mort."[2] [my emphasis]

A peasant woman from the village you see between these two mountains . . . sent her husband to her family's home, in a neighboring hamlet. This unfortunate man was killed there by one of his brothers-in-law. The next day I went to the house where the accident had taken place. There *I saw a tableau*, and

---

A portion of this chapter is reprinted, with permission, from *L'Esprit Créateur* 24, no. 1 (1984): 99-107.

heard a speech that I have not forgotten. The dead man was stretched out on a bed. His naked legs hung over the bed. His disheveled wife was on the ground. She held her husband's feet; *and she said while breaking into tears, and so movingly that she drew tears from everyone*: "Alas! when I sent you here, I didn't think these feet would lead you to death."

Now Dorval may present this tableau as perfect theatrical material, but one suspects that as a staged scene it would have lost most of the force it conveys as a narration. Why is this the case? Does the tableau work precisely insofar as it lends itself not to the stage but to the theater of one's imagination?

When Diderot speaks of the tableau, he presents it as a moment when narrative action comes to a halt. For example, when Dorval's interlocutor in the *Entretiens, Moi,* contrasts the sudden turns of fortune that French Classical theater called *coups de théâtre* with the painterly composition of the tableau:

> *Un incident qui se passe en action*, et qui change subitement l'état des personnages, est un coup de théâtre. *Une disposition des personnages* sur la scène, si naturelle et vraie, que, rendue fidèlement par un peintre, elle me plairait sur la toile, est un tableau.[3] [My emphasis]

> *An incident which takes place in action*, and which suddenly changes the characters' situation is a *coup de théâtre. A disposition of the characters* on stage, which is so natural and true that, faithfully rendered by a painter, it would please me on canvas, is a tableau.

In theory, then, the tableau is a narrative device and a dialogic one, too. As critics have frequently noted, Diderot's discourse seeks to define itself in terms of an absent interlocutor.[4] And his tableaux are no exception to this rule: like the rest of Diderot's text, they orient themselves toward the discourse of an absent interlocutor, the figure whom Michael Fried has aptly termed the "beholder." Fried has argued quite convincingly that French painting of Diderot's time tends to neutralize the presence of the beholder. We shall see, however, that the absence of the beholder is so crucial to the structure of Diderot's written tableaux that we must speak of the beholder as a character in it. Indeed, the insistent presence of the beholder will reveal itself to be quite complex. In the tableau cited above, the peasant woman's tears speak to her beholders, who "answer" them with tears of their own, thereby repeating her gesture.

This last detail points to a third, formal aspect of the tableau, namely its iterability. Consider another tableau from the *Entretiens*, which also has the form of a narrative:

MOI. Le beau tableau, car c'en est un, ce me semble, que le malheureux Clairville, renversé sur le sein de son ami, comme dans le seul asile qui lui reste.
DORVAL. Vous pensez bien à sa peine, mais vous oubliez la mienne. Que ce moment fut cruel pour moi!
MOI. Je le sais, je le sais. Je me souviens que tandis qu'il exhalait sa plainte et sa douleur, vous versiez des larmens sur lui. *Ce ne sont pas là des circonstances qui s'oublient.*[5] [My emphasis]

MOI. What a fine tableau, for it seems one to me, was the unhappy Clairville, leaning on his friend's breast, as if in the only refuge left to him.
DORVAL. You easily imagine his sorrow, but you forget mine. How cruel this moment was for me!
MOI. I know, I know. I remember that while he gave vent to his sorrow and pain, you were shedding tears on him. *Such circumstances as these are not easily forgotten.*

The dialogic relations are more complex here than in the first example: Clairville is speaking to Dorval and making him cry, while the tableau that they form in turn produces its effect upon *Moi*, the beholder. The whole scene, remarks *Moi*, is eminently repeatable: "Such circumstances as these are not easily forgotten." A tableau makes an impression upon the beholder, it leaves a mark (a memory trace) on him. The beholder, in turn, then relives (that is, rewrites) the impression by recounting it religiously: "Je gagerais presque que, dans la quatrième scène du second acte, il n'y a pas un mot qui ne soit vrai. Elle m'a désolé dans le salon, et j'ai pris un plaisir infini à lire."[6] ["I would almost wager that, in the fourth scene of the second act, there is not a word which isn't true. It saddened me in the salon, and I took infinte pleasure in reading it."] In fact, the entire text of *Le Père de famille* is a simulated transcript of real events that is meant to be re-enacted annually by the participants—even though (or maybe more accurately, *because*) the *père de famille* himself has since died.[7]

By repeating a gesture represented in the tableau, the beholder testifies to a double partiality. He shows himself to be partial, first, by taking sides with the represented characters, by espousing their cause, as it were. Second, the beholder plays what is literally a part, a fragment; he aims to replace a part that the tableau has lost. In the tableau of the grieving peasant woman, it is her late husband who is missing—he is the absent part. Moreover, that missing part is represented in the tableau by parts of his body (legs, feet) and by his widow's tears. These fragments point to what has been lost and also seek to conjure away that loss: as if by accumulating partial images, one could suggest that the tableau is and always has been whole.

This combination of paradoxical denial (*Verneinung, dénégation*) or suspension of that loss in a fixed image defines the fetishistic operation. In psychoanalysis, the fetish is a means of denying that woman has no phallus, while also implicitly admitting it. Deleuze's account of the genesis and structure of the fetish is most appropriate to our understanding of the tableau:

> Le fétichiste élirait comme fétiche le dernier objet qu'il a vu, enfant, avant de s'apercevoir de l'absence (la chaussure, par exemple, pour un regard qui remonte à partir du pied); et le retour à cet objet, à ce point de départ, lui permettrait de maintenir en droit l'existence de l'organe contesté. Le fétiche ne serait donc nullement un symbole, mais comme *un plan fixe et figé, une image arrêtée, une photo à laquelle on reviendrait toujours pour conjurer les suites fâcheuses du mouvement.* . . . [I]l représenterait le dernier moment où l'on pouvait encore croire . . .[8] [My emphasis]

> The fetishist's choice of a fetish is determined by the last object he saw as a child before becoming aware of the missing penis (a shoe, for example, in the case of a glance directed from the feet upwards). The constant return to this object, this point of departure, enables him to validate the existence of the organ that is in dispute. The fetish is therefore not a symbol at all, but as it were *a frozen, arrested, two-dimensional image, a photograph to which one returns repeatedly to exorcise the dangerous consequences of movement.* . . . [I]t represents the last point at which it was still possible to believe . . .

One could surely pursue the psychoanalytic meaning of the tableau, notably in regard to its masochistic identification of the beholder with the victim. Here I would like only to emphasize that the tableau in Diderot is a sort of fetishistic snapshot in which the transitoriness of the real world is magically transformed into an ideal fixity.

If one were to make a list of the fetishized parts of this tableau, one would have to include not only the dead man's legs and feet, as well as his widow's hair (the word *échevelée* regularly appears in Diderot's evocations of suffering female virtue)—which are the sort of fetishistic object-choices that psychoanalytic literature would lead us to expect—but also every last bit of narrative detail. Since this tableau is narrated rather than staged, it cannot give tangible reality to a whole scene but must present fragments of that scene and endow them with an ideal power, which is then made available to the beholder's imagination. In general terms, the tableau depends upon the power of fragments to invest the imagination, the ability of a part (which psychoanalysis calls the fetish) to make an ideal whole (the phallus). In particular, I would note the fetishistic character of the quotation that concludes this particular tableau ("Je ne pensais pas que ces pieds te menaient à la mort"). The gesture of quotation isolates a piece of discourse, as one might cut off a lock of hair, thereby both marking it as a repetition of another piece and removing that fragment from the contingency of any particular context. At another level, moreover, this gesture is duplicated within the quotation itself by the figure of synecdoche, a part for a whole: "Je ne pensais pas que *ces pieds* te menaient à la mort." [My emphasis]

The fragmented tableau and its component parts have the same fetishistic structure. Each is in some sense a part of an ideal whole that would immediately vanish if one tried to make it whole by actually staging it. Because they play upon imaginary wholes, Diderot's tableaux were bound to fail as theatrical devices, whereas their narrative summaries nearly always possess a disquieting intensity. That intensity depends upon the dialogic appeal to the partiality of the beholder, ethically and aesthetically. It asks the beholder to be partial to the suffering of the represented characters, and thereby also to define himself as the missing part or fragment that the tableau has not really lost, at least ideally. All of the actors in the dialogic relationship that defines the tableau share a certain partiality or partialness: the author or maker, the represented characters, and the beholder or remaker all take sides, and all are parts of an incomplete whole. This partiality is dialogic in that each actor addresses herself or himself to what another appears to have lost. She or he "addresses" the self, not only as one orients one's discourse toward an interlocutor but also as one addresses a letter to someone. He or she may be said to be destined for another, destined to compensate for a loss that the tableau both represents and negates. It is on paper, not on the stage, that Diderot's tableaux have the power to move the beholder.

On paper there is a partial, fragmented representation. Yet throughout numerous changes of situation and character, one fundamental figure defines its subject: a loss in the family. One sees a widowed peasant woman whose husband has been killed, and by her own brother; "a mother" or "a father"[9] mourning the loss of a son; another mother (who only happens to be *Queen* Clytemnestra) torn by sorrow because her husband has resolved to sacrifice their daughter. They are bereaved family members or, as in this tableau from the *Père de famille*, persons suddenly without a family: Clairville seeking solace for his unrequited love on the shoulder of his friend and rival, for example. Or the heroine of *La Religieuse*, whose pathetic tableaux show her repeatedly suffering at the hands of evil mothers and fathers. Whether it depicts Queen Clytemnestra bewailing the imminent loss of Iphigenia or just an "épouse tendre,"[10] the tableau represents the family *at a loss*, so to speak, in mourning for a parent or child.

This loss appears both at the level of the representation (showing a widow, a venerable old man, and so forth) and at the level of the dialogic relationship between that representation and its beholder. As we shall see, the loss that the tableau represents is meant to be made good by the beholder, who must supply the loss by supplementing or standing in for the missing family member. The beholder's (ontological) presence is required. A suffering, fragmented family requires another fragment, the beholder, to be whole. To play that part, the beholder has to pay the price of self-sacrifice. To espouse a just cause is to become partial, in both senses of that word.

As Diderot put it in the *Eloge de Richardson*, "Virtue . . . is a self-sacrifice."[11] The beholder's tear repeats the sacrifices that the represented characters have made and also represents the beholder's own sacrifice. In the dialogic structure of the tableau, tears perform a triple function corresponding to three formal properties of the tableau noted above: they *relate* a sacrifice, *repeat* it, and *represent* or *signal* it. Whoever sheds the tears (be it author, characters, or beholder), a sacrifice is being narrated and signified, and never for the first time (always as a re-presentation). The dialogue of these three instances (author, character, beholder) makes that sacrifice, makes the tableau. Virtue requires a sacrificial representation—it requires a tableau.

The interplay of these discursive instances defines the tableau, which has no existence independent of their dialogue. Collectively, these three parts make the tableau; they are its fragmentary and collective subject. Not only do these instances make the tableau, they also represent themselves. They are doubly the subject of the tableau, its maker and its topic, just as the family relationships that the tableau represents are repeated in the relationships among author, characters, and beholder. The sacrifice of this collective subject detaches the tableau and its component parts from the contingency of their context and places each within quotation marks. Within its context, each part is incomplete, just as the author, the tableau, and the beholder are incomplete in their contexts. Yet when the parts enter into dialogue with one another, they ideally become as one body, like communicants joined in the Eucharist. At least in theory.

This sacrificial dialogue has something intensely erotic about it. In the tableau with which I began, the juxtaposition of a widow's "disheveled" hair with the naked legs and feet of her husband's cadaver achieves its effect through interplay between the aura of piety that surrounds the scene of bereavement and the transgression that the piety calls forth. On the one hand, this tableau offers sublimity by inviting the beholder to sympathize with an ethically moving spectacle; on the other, the very misfortunes of this widow in mourning strangely become her. Her acquaintance with death would become her, according to Bataille's L'Erotisme, precisely because of the prohibition associated with death.[12] This tableau is ethically, and *therefore* erotically moving, a perversity that is too frequently overlooked. Once one has recognized this erotic dimension of the tableau, it becomes difficult to view the device as simply a maudlin appeal to middle-class values.[13] Awareness of this eroticism, in Bataille's sense, helps one to understand just what Diderot meant when he spoke of the "plaisir de s'attendrir et de répandre des larmes" ["the pleasure of being moved and shedding tears"].[14]

Another example of this strange eroticism can be observed in Diderot's inaccurate account of a scene from Lillo's middle-class drama, *The London Merchant*. In act 5 of the play there is a scene where the repentant hero, who has been driven to crime by an unrepentant prostitute, encounters this woman at the gallows where he is about to be hanged. In an earlier scene of this same act, Barnwell (the hero) receives a visit in his prison cell from his chaste beloved, who also happens to be his employer's daughter. Paul Vernière suggested that Diderot inadvertently substituted the prison scene for the gallows scene when he wrote: "La maîtresse de Barnevelt [sic] entre *échevelée* dans la prison de son amant. Les deux amis s'ambarasent et tombent à terre."[15] [My emphasis] ["Barnwell's mistress enters *disheveled* into her lover's prison. The two friends embrace and fall to the ground."] Peter Szondi, on the other hand, believed that Diderot had confused not the two scenes but the two women, by replacing Barnwell's innocent beloved with the depraved Millwood.[16] Neither critic sought to interpret this mistake, or to explain why Diderot has the couple fall to the ground ("[ils] tombent à terre"), which happens in neither scene. On the other hand, there is a scene in act 5 of *The London Merchant* in which Barnwell and the (male) friend whose trust he has betrayed *do* fall to the ground and embrace, but this scene the critics do not mention. I shall return to this homosexual bond below. Whether or not they were intentional, these changes that Diderot made in Lillo's text testify to the strong erotic impulse behind much Enlightenment moralizing.[17]

The sensuous moralism of a Diderot or a Greuze, for example, relies upon the ironic juxtaposition of an ethical prohibition and its transgression. By excluding grieving widows, loving mothers, and virgins as objects of desire, moral law invites its own transgression. In fact, the pathos that sets these prohibited objects apart signals their desirability. The more pathetically a figure is represented, the more it has been subject to prohibition and hence becomes desirable. It is not surprising, then, that the most highly sentimentalized relationships in Diderot are those between parents and children. In these family relationships, at once erotic and pathetic, Diderot's dialogue locates the kinship between sexual reproduction and death. A loss in the family engenders the tableau, and that loss will have to be overcome by the beholder.

So Szondi was not quite right to claim that Diderot's tableaux depict reconciliation [*Versöhnung*],[18] the family again made whole. These tableaux express a desire for reconciliation, a desire to make up for what the family has lost. However, that loss or absence is always implicitly replaced by a silent beholder who identifies with the suffering of the virtuous family members and must vicariously fill in for those who have departed. In this manner, what has been sacrificed in a now-fragmented family—the missing part—reappears *outside* the tableau in the figure of the beholder. When he sees the tableau (and I use the masculine pronoun advisedly), the beholder makes a sacrifice equivalent to the original one, to the "making sacred" of a family member. In so doing, the beholder repeats the gesture of the tableau's maker (the author), which frequently has already been repeated by the represented characters (for example: "Je me souviens que, tandis qu'il exhalait sa plainte et sa douleur, vous versiez des larmes sur lui").[19] Just as the (re)maker of the tableau is absent, so the tableau itself represents an absence: the part (that of the writer or beholder) that is missing.

Every representation implies a viewer or beholder, but the tableau posits a specific relationship to the beholder. There is a desire that this loss in the family that was at the origin of the tableau be mourned and compensated for by the beholder whom the tableau summons forth. The family, which had been broken apart, is to be reconstituted at another level. In that case, the family would be reborn from its own ashes at the level of general solidarity between one human being and another. The family's fragmentation would once again be made whole at the level of the family of Man. Ideally, this dialectical recovery would take place were it not that these two levels (the representation, the beholder), these two parts of the tableau's *subject*, never completely overlap. To be whole, each part of the subject requires precisely what it lacks, namely, the other; each requires the very absence that has caused it to be. Just as the tableau exists by virtue of the family member who has been excluded from its frame (who is absent), so the sympathetic beholder owes his existence *as beholder* to that exclusion.

For him really to enter the representational frame, the beholder would have to make a sacrifice that is not just symbolic (not just tears); he would have to imitate the absent family member by actually sacrificing himself.[20] Even then, the beholder would only have shuttled from one part of the subject, that of its (re)maker, to the subject as topic, thereby summoning forth yet another beholder's part. A desire for wholeness never alters the fact that the tableau is always incomplete. The tableau is always minus one. Diderot's written tableaux are therefore structured quite differently from the contemporary paintings that Michael Fried has so brilliantly analyzed. In the written tableau, a loss inside the tableau constitutes the beholder outside it.

This structural fragmentation never fails to move the beholder to tears. Upon occasion, as when the widowed peasant woman breaks into tears and speaks—"avec une action qui en arrachait à tout le monde" ["in a way that drew tears from everyone]—the beholder's tears are literally torn out of him. These sacrificial fragments are important not only in terms of structure, but also in terms of time and history. In several ways, tears convey the relationship between a certain absence (what is presently lacking) and a certain presence (the wholeness that was or that ought to be), between a present that has been torn apart and a future where all will have been mended. The family used to be whole, yet it is fragmented; its members are virtuous, and therefore ought to be happy, but they are not.[21] The fatherly beholder ought to be able to make up for that absence, a united Family of Man should supersede the fragmented nuclear family, but they never quite do. There ought to be, there *must* be a Heavenly Father up there, in whose eyes this sacrifice has a meaning. All men will become brothers because, as Schiller wrote in the *Ode to Joy*, "In der Sternenzelt muss ein lieber Vater wohnen" ["In the firmament a dear Father must abide"].

Peter Szondi cited a passage in Lessing's correspondence that underlies the importance, in the rhetoric of pathos, of playing upon the difference between present unhappiness and the happiness that ought to be. "A few months before the appearance of *Le Fils naturel*," wrote Szondi, "in a letter of 29 November 1756 to Friedrich Nicolai, Lessing distinguished 'three degrees of pity and compassion, tears being the middle degree . . .:

> Emotion is aroused when I clearly conceive neither the perfections [*Vollkommenheiten*] nor the ill luck involved in the case, but rather have only an obscure notion of both; the sight of every beggar, for example, moves me in this way. He draws tears from me only when he makes me better acquainted with his good qualities as well as with his misfortunes, and, in fact, with both *simultaneously*, which is the real trick of eliciting tears.' "22

Both "perfections" and "ill luck" must be shown if the beholder is to cry, and these must not appear too clearly ("only an obscure notion of both").

The phantasy-like tableau also depends upon this vague quality. It must play upon the "exquisite difference"23 between these two levels in order to produce its characteristic aesthetic effect, "the sweet pleasure of being moved and shedding tears." As in Lessing, that pleasure will be made more exquisite still by the difference, implicit in Lessing's example, between the beholder's fortune and that of the represented characters. On the one hand, the beholder must witness the happiness that ought to obtain in the (nuclear) family, if only everyone inside and outside of the family were virtuous; on the other, he has to see the sacrifices, the violence at the origin of the family. Nothing must suggest that one could preclude the other, that there might be a causal relationship between the beholder's prosperity and the misery he witnesses, or between his own isolation and the fragmented family before him. If tears are to remain a satisfying response to the situation, the beholder must have the impression of just happening upon unfortunate fellow members of the human family. In this case, the sacrifice of a tear will be quite enough.

Whether or not this social sacrifice is thematized (as social, in Lessing's example; or as sacrifice in Diderot's reference in Racine's *Iphigénie*), the tableau and the tears it elicits represent both a loss and a desire to compensate for that loss in ideal form. Beneath the gaze of a benevolent, paternal figure, social conflicts disappear, social relations are momentarily both repaired and arrested; that is, they are *fixed*. At this level, the dialogic structure of the tableau provides a classic example of ideology in the Marxian sense: with the shedding of a tear, the conflictual nature of social life is conjured away.

Yet the dialogic meaning of these tears is even more complex. When the virtuous bourgeois cries, he addresses not only the less fortunate members of the Third Estate but also the nobility, as well as the "opposite sex" in general. Those tears may look silly to a cold-hearted aristocrat,[24] but they betray a rich interior drama that only a real man could experience: "La larme qui s'échappe de l'homme vraiment homme nous touche plus que tous les pleurs d'une femme."[25] ["The tear which escapes from a really manly man touches us more than all a woman's weeping."] A virile *larme* has nothing theatrical about it, and so it touches the beholder (*nous*), who knows through experience what that tear has cost him. "Chaque ligne de *L'Homme de qualité retiré du monde, du Doyen de Killerine* et de *Cleveland*," writes Diderot, "excite en moi un mouvement d'intérêt sur les malheurs de la vertu, et me coûte des larmes."[26] ["Every line of *L'Homme de qualité retiré du monde*, of the *Doyen de Killerine* and of *Cleveland*, excites in me a movement of interest in the misfortunes of virtue, and costs me tears."] When the bourgeois cries, not only does he give testimony to his own sensitivity, but those tears reveal his (and the beholder's) participation in human nature, his "virtue." That virtue, in turn, provides him with a natural right to economic and political power; after all, it suggests, at the head of the family there ought to be someone who really cares for his children. For virtue to reign supreme, the necessary sacrifices will have to be made. These are the sacrifices that the represented characters eternally repeat, as well as those that its author and subsequent beholders have made and will make. As agent and as topic, the subject of the tableau is being sacrificed.

The tableau is also a *tombeau* [tomb]. Like the tomb of a dead soldier, it recalls the sacrifices that have been made for a virtuous cause (in this case, for the cause of virtue) and urges the beholder to emulate the model. At once it marks a loss and promises the future redemption of that loss, as if the permanence of the aesthetic object could somehow be imparted to the entire human family—past and present—in a future without loss, without suffering, even without death. This is precisely why so many losses and so much suffering are necessary right now. This *tableau-tombeau* asks the beholder to be prepared to make whatever sacrifices may be necessary, either of oneself or of others. Later in the century, this logic would inspire the paintings of David and the speeches of Robespierre. In any case, the temporal structure of the tableau is also sacrificial: an unhappy present is sacrificed to a happy future; what is, to what ought to be, to what someday will be. In the tableau, everything lacking in the present social order is buried. It is as if the tableau were a monument to the fulfillment that virtue ought to have brought, and that surely it will bring. That fulfillment, which depends upon the future sacrifices of virtuous, paternal onlookers, takes shape in the future anterior: from the viewpoint of that future onlooker, the present loss in the family *will have been* redeemed.

Elsewhere Diderot imagines this monumentalized future anterior in the figure of the statue. For example, in *Le Neveu de Rameau*, where *Moi* contends that unrecognized genius will someday achieve recognition in statue form: "On leur élève des statues et on les regarde comme les beinfaiteurs du genre humain."[27] ["They put up statues to them and call them benefactors of the race."] In the statue, a life that once seemed to have been going to waste has been conserved. But at stake in the argument between *Moi* and *Lui* over artistic genius is not only a general contradiction between the ethical and the aesthetic levels, between the good man and the great artist, but the specific contradiction between the great artist and the happiness of his family. The "great" Rameau, according to *Moi*,

> est un homme dur; c'est un brutal; il est sans humanité; il
> est avare. Il est mauvais père, mauvais époux; mauvais oncle;
> mais il n'est pas assez décidé que ce soit un homme de génie.[28]

> is a hard man, brutal, inhuman, miserly, a bad father, bad
> husband, and bad uncle. And it is by no means sure that he is a
> genius.

But if history has not yet turned in a verdict on Rameau's genius, says *Lui*, what about Racine or Voltaire?

> Lequel des deux préfériez-vous? ou qu'il eût été un bon homme,
> faisant régulièrement tous les ans un enfant légitime à sa femme,
> bon mari; bon père, bon oncle, bon voisin, honnête commer-
> çant, mais rien de plus; ou qu'il eût été fourbe, traître,
> ambitieux, envieux, méchant; mais auteur d'*Andromaque*, de
> *Britannicus*, d'*Iphigénie*, de *Phèdre*, d'*Athalie*.[29]

> Well, which would you prefer—that he should have been a good
> soul, . . . legitimately getting his wife with child annually—
> a good husband, good father, good uncle, good neighbor,
> fair trader and nothing more; or that he should have been de-
> ceitful, disloyal, ambitious, envious, and mean, but also

the creator of *Andromaque, Britannicus, Iphigénie, Phèdre,* and *Athalie*?

He who today looks like a bad father may someday be recognized as a great artist. In the future, it will appear that the sacrifices he has made have not been in vain, that his life has not been wasted. What the Nephew cynically reduces to meaningless waste ("O stercus pretiosum") will then turn out to have engendered eternal significance: "De Racine méchant, que restera-t-il? Rien. De Racine homme homme de génie? L'ouvrage est éternal."[30] ["Of Racine the wicked man, what will remain? And Racine the genius? His work is eternal."] What now appears as pure waste, as *stercus*, will later have become all that really mattered. Racine may have made the people around him suffer: "Il a fait souffrir quelques êtres qui ne sont plus; auxquels nous ne prenons presqu'aucun intérêt."[31] ["He brought suffering on a few persons who who are dead and in whom we take no interest."] But the sacrifices of the past have been redeemed by the recognition of this genius: "Cet homme n'a été bon que pour des inconnus, et que pour le temps où il était plus."[32] ["The fellow was of use only to people he didn't know, at a time when he had ceased to live."] The process by which sacrifices imposed by a genius upon those around him are later redeemed finds its most memorable expression in the organic figure of a tree:

C'est un arbre qui a fait sécher quelques arbres plantés dans son voisinage; qui a étouffé les plantes qui croissaient à ses pieds; mais il a porté sa cime jusque dans la nue; ses branches se sont étendues au loin.[33]

He is a tree which has stunted a few trees in his vicinage and blighted the plants growing at his feet; but his topmost branch reached the sky; his boughs spread afar.

Unlike the inorganic images of the statue or tableau, the figure of the tree displays temporal and spatial relations to the past, to that time when its contributions to humanity were not yet recognized. Its very shape shows the viewer what sacrifices have been made and why they have been worth it. A thousand years from now, the sacrifices Racine imposed upon those around him will be redeemed by the *tears* and admiration of the entire human race.[34] Unlike the inorganic, artistic figure of future anteriority, the tree plunges its roots into the past whose fulfillment it is. In different ways, each of these images expresses the redemption that will eventually be granted to the truth and to its genial representatives from the transcendent viewpoint of humanity as a whole:

Oublions pour un moment le point que nous occupons dans
l'espace et dans la durée; et étendons notre vue sur les siècles à
venir, les régions les plus éloignées, et les peuples à naître.[35]

Forget for a moment the point we occupy in time and space,
and project your vision into centuries to come, into the
most remote places, and nations yet unborn.

Viewed from the perspective of generations as yet unborn, the sacrifices of an individual's family will not appear to have been losses at
all. While a tree displays a continuous relationship between past and
present, a tableau repeats a break in the past. Whatever sacrifices a
great shade tree has required have not been its own, whereas a tableau
makes another sacrifice as it recapitulates a sacred moment of the
past, when the wholeness of the family was lost. Precisely because a
tree is not a representation, but an organism to which meaning may
be attached, it bears the traces of a continuous relationship to its
own past. A tableau re-presents, and what it represents is not its own
past but the past of its subject (topic, agent). On the other hand, because it is a work of art the tableau has its place in a network of filia-
tion, in a genealogical "tree." Because it displays an organic link between past and present, the tree is an apt figure for a genealogy; but
it bears no traces of its genealogy or origins except in its seeds, that
is, in its own future. In the tree, there is a continuous, organic link
with a past whose origins are unknown, whereas the tableau posits a
break or loss *in* the past as the basis for its continuity *with* the past.

In Diderot's examples, the artist's works eventually compensate
for whatever he may have lacked as a father, in the future moment
when the beholders of those works recognize in the artist's image a
model of human achievement. In this moment of recognition, a new
generation of beholders will be engendered: grandchildren, great-
grandchildren, and so on. Just as to identify oneself with a character
is to recognize oneself in them, so to recognize the greatness of the
author one has to recognize oneself, one's virtue, in the author's
children and hence to recognize one's fraternity or kinship with the
author. When that recognition reaches universal dimensions, then all
men will have become brothers, and the human family will have become one. Thus to recognize oneself in the author means to anticipate
one's recognition in the eyes of future generations: as if the moral
qualities that allow the beholder to be moved by a loss in the family
would some day turn to his advantage; as if the peculiar aptitude to
shed tears over such representations made the beholder worthy of

himself being recognized in the minds and monuments of future generations.

How could Diderot achieve such recognition? How could he move his readers or beholders to tears? Certainly not within the stuffy *bienséances* of French Classicism, which required that all representations of violence and death be banished from the stage. Diderot's passionate temperament was hardly compatible with official ideas of theatrical decorum, as Chouillet and Szondi have argued.[36] Chouillet portrayed Diderot as a genius without an audience, an artist who did not dare to write and stage a play that had the violent intensity of his own convictions. In addition, he suggested that the "canevas tragique" [tragic outline] for *Le Fils naturel* that Dorval reveals during the *Entretiens* provides a clue to the tragedy that Diderot would have liked to write.[37] This may well be the case, although Vernière and Szondi contended, rather less charitably, that this version of the play is not really tragic, but rather "du mauvais mélodrame."[38] Whether one reads his play as potential tragedy or as poor melodrama, the fact that it concludes by Dorval's putting an end to his own life certainly supports a reading of Diderot's pathos as sacrificial dialogue.

Chapter Two
Genealogy of the Beholder

In the previous chapter, I argued that Diderot's writings display a series of shifts in emphasis: first, that despite the philosophe's advocacy of the tableau as part of a program for theatrical reform, his most powerful tableaux are meant to be read and not staged; second, that the same is true of his dialogues, that they are not well suited to staging; and third, that the fundamental dialogue in Diderot takes place not really between characters, but among the author, the printed dialogue of these characters, and the possible responses of the reader or "beholder." In this chapter, I shall develop an interpretation of the *kinship* among the participants in Diderot's sacrificial dialogue.

In *Le Fils naturel*, Rosalie and Dorval are drawn to each other by a love that neither will admit to; Clairville also loves Rosalie, although she does not believe she loves him, and his sister Constance's love for Dorval is also unrequited. All the unrequited desires are known, but the reciprocal desires are kept silent. As Chouillet notes, if the truth should come out, then "tragedy" is possible.[1] Through efforts of will, however, Constance and Dorval forestall a possible unhappy ending until the moment when old Lysimond returns at the end of act 5 and recognizes in Dorval his "natural son" and in Rosalie his daughter. Nearly simultaneously ("presque au même instant"), Rosalie and Dorval discover who they really are:

ROSALE.   Mon frère!
DORVAL.   Ma soeur!
ROSALIE.   Dorval!
DORVAL.   Rosalie!   (Ces mots se disent avec
                                   toute la vitesse de la
                                   surprise et se font entendre
                                   presque au même instant.)[2]

ROSALIE.   My brother!
DORVAL.   My sister!
ROSALIE.   Dorval!
DORVAL.   Rosalie!   (These words are spoken
                                   with the speed of surprise
                                   and are heard at almost the
                                   same instant.)

What drew Rosalie and Dorval together, it now turns out, was not really passion but blood; conflicts that had threatened to tear a family apart are resolved at the moment when that family recognizes itself as such, under the eye of a loving father.

The similarities between this moment of recognition in a model *drame* and the parallel moment in Sophocles' model tragedy *Oedipus the King* are as significant as the differences between them. In both cases, the son finally discovers who he is by seeing who his father is. In the Greek tragedy, the hero is blinded by the recognition that his father is the man he killed long before at a crossroads and that his mother is his wife. The effect of this representation upon the audience, of course, is the much-debated catharsis or purge of pity and fear; the *drame*, however, aims to move its audience to tears of delight at the moment when its hero recognizes that the father whom he thought dead is now alive and, moreover, that the woman he secretly wanted to marry is really his sister. In Sophocles, this revelation is tragic news, whereas in Diderot it is cause for celebration. Just as Oedipus is horrified to learn that his wife is his mother, so Dorval is relieved to learn that his secret love is his sister. In one case, incestuous desire is a reason for horror; in the other, it causes rejoicing. More precisely stated, in *Le Fils naturel*[3] the desire that seemed to have encountered a rival desire is shown not to have had a rival at all. The love is not amorous and therefore incestuous, but fraternal after all.

Yet this news does not just make things right. Both Dorval and the audience now realize that they have been believing that a brother and sister were in love with each other, they have been giving credence to what (it now appears) would have been an incestuous desire if they had been right to believe it an amorous desire. There might have been a tragedy here. This *drame* has a curious way of playing upon the contrast between the incestuous, violent horror of what might have been and the normative satisfaction of what is. Diderot was, of course, not the only writer of his period to put incest to dramatic effect, but only he evokes the possibility of incest in this retroactive, unsettling way.[4] We thought that there was conflict between two men over a woman, but that conflict never really existed except in their and our imagination. What might have been is so immoral, and what is, so moral, that in the moment of recognition Dorval and his audience are treated to the exquisite difference between the two.

Once again, losses in the past are redeemed by the appearance of the father. Rather than revealing the fact of incest, *Le Fils naturel* asserts first that there never really was any incest, and second that there might well have been. For an instant, the present serves as a pleasant alibi for imagining what might have been. We have already noticed the importance in Diderot of interplay between the ethical and the erotic. We may also observe now that this interplay is mediated by a certain notion of the family. Dorval and his audience can imagine the possibility of having had incestuous desires, but there really has been no desire that is forbidden by paternal law. The Father finally comes on stage, he finally comes home, and at that very moment the beholder realizes that there might have been an incest and, that there was none. Returning to a position he has never really ceased to occupy, the Father simultaneously opens up and forecloses the possibility of incest, while revealing that he has not been dead, after all, but just away from home. Since everyone finally is at home and reunited, desires that might have been forbidden may now be fulfilled.

All this supposedly happened, Diderot tells us, during the real events upon which the play is based, but it never happened during even the first performance of the play. *Le Fils naturel* presents itself as a kind of "docudrama," as the recreation of events that once took place among real people. The cast of characters lists both the participants in the drama (Dorval, et al.) and the professional actors who took over their roles at the first public performance ("les noms des personnages réels de la pièce, avec ceux des acteurs qui pourraient les remplacer") ["the names of the real characters of the play, with those of the actors who could replace them"]. Moreover, we are told in the "Histoire véritable de la pièce" that these real people actually replayed the events one year later, in obedience to the wishes of Lysimond, the Father, who had since died.

This performance would have had no audience but the performers, had *Moi* not been invited. Lysimond asks his son Dorval to put these real events into the form of a play, and Dorval answers elliptically: "Une pièce, mon père₁" To which his father responds: "Oui, mon enfant:

> Il ne s'agit point d'élever ici des tréteaux, mais de conserver la mémoire d'un événement qui nous touche, et de la rendre comme il s'est passé. . . . Nous le renouvellerions nous-mêmes, tous les ans, dans cette maison, dans ce salon. Les choses que nous avons dites, nous les redirions. Tes enfants en feraient autant, et les leurs, et leurs descendants. Et je me survivrais à moi-même, et j'irais converser ainsi, d,'âge en âge, avec tous mes neveux. . . . Dorval, penses-tu, qu'un ouvrage qui leur transmettrait nos propres idées, les discours que nous avons tenus dans une des circonstances les plus importantes de notre vie, ne valût mieux que des portraits de famille qui ne montrent de nous qu'un moment de notre visage.[5]

> It is not a matter here of staging a play, but of conserving the memory of an event which touches us, and of rendering it as it happened. . . . We should renew it ourselves every year, in this house, in this room. The things we said, we should repeat. Your children would do as much, and theirs, and their descendants. And I should survive myself, and I should thus go on conversing, from age to age, with all my descendants. . . . Dorval, do you think that a work which would transmit to them our own ideas, the speeches we made in one of the most important circumstances of our life, would not be worth more than family portraits which show only a single moment of our face.

As neither the play's author nor simply its recorder, Dorval has a curious role to play in the play which bears his name. The play has no author, in fact, since it is supposedly only the redramatization of real events, but it is not the transcript of those events, either. Whatever the precise nature of Dorval's contribution, it was done out of filial duty (Celui qui l'a commandée n'est plus")[6] ["He who ordered it is no more"]. The result of this dramatization will be worth more than family portraits ("[Il] valût mieux que des portraits de famille") because it will manage to reconcile the passage of time with timelessness, diachrony with synchrony. Unlike other theatrical performances, for example, this one would have no other audience than the participants in the original events, who would also be the actors ("une

pièce . . . que nous représenterions entre nous") ["a play . . .
which we should perform among ourselves"]. At least in principle,
nothing will have been lost, at least in the first performance; and
even (or especially) thereafter (in the future) nothing will have been
lost either, since it will bring generations past, present, and future into conversation with each other.

As actors, members of the family would immortalize events in their
past and themselves as participants in those events. They would immortalize themselves by momentarily sacrificing their present identity to reproduce an image of what they once had been. By playing a
part once a year, they would therefore act out their own passing,
mortal nature. They would represent their own mortality in the hope
of overcoming it. Likewise, by becoming the play's makers, its performers, and its beholders, they would hope to overcome the inherent
dialogic differences among those parts. The impossibility of suppressing all dialogic difference will soon be prefigured by the death of
Lysimond, whose role will have to be played by someone else. In any
case, that absence will always have been structurally prefigured by
the very possibility of playing a part, whether that of author, actor,
or beholder. In the same fashion, the presence of an extra character
(*Moi*) at the play's first performance answers to the absence of
Lysimond and also represents the built-in presence of a beholder's
part. Later on, that part will be played by Lysimond's descendants
("mes neveux"), who will be asked to compensate for the loss that
the play presupposes. Like the character of Lysimond in act 5, the
beholder is asked to make the family whole once again. When the
real father, Lysimond, supposedly dies before the first performance,
his death carries out the logic of the play: since the Father is no
longer present (at home), someone else must play his role. Of course,
it will turn out that, however much this other person resembles the
Father, he cannot ever quite replace him.[7]

Given the realistic, "documentary" impulse behind *Le Fils naturel*
—the desire to reproduce words, gestures, and feelings exactly as
they originally were—the play has a decidedly religious, ritualistic
character. *Le Fils naturel* is designed as a commemorative ritual to be
repeated annually on the date of the original events. It is as if the
middle-class drama, by contesting the hierarchical basis of theater in
the ancien régime, had reinvented the ritualistic origins of theater. The
tableau (which reconciles synchrony and diachrony in the imagination)
was according to Szondi[8] an anti-*coup de théâtre*, the very emblem
of middle-class rationality. Here it assumes an essentially hieratic
form (its component parts so many traits drawn and temporarily

fixed, monumentalized by the participants' bodies), as the entire play acts out a ritual of origins.

As a matter of fact, one is struck by the resemblance between Diderot's tableaux and the pageants that E. K. Chambers described in *The Mediaeval Stage.*[9] According to Chambers, it was probably in conjunction with the ceremonies of Corpus Christi day that persons would mount elaborate floats as part of a procession that involved a series of "stations." In beholding these silent "*tableaux,*"[10] the Christian was enjoined to cry: first, over one's own mortality; second, over the guilt felt at Christ's death; and third, because the very capacity to be moved by Christ's Passion redeemed the Christian in the eyes of God. In medieval terms, these tears blinded the eyes of the Christian's sensuous self so that the spiritual self might contemplate spiritual reality. Moreover, belief in the dual nature of man prevented this moment of self-blinding from producing a Christian version of that sudden void that marked the moment of Greek catharsis: the Christian cried, not at tragedy, but at a sort of *drame.*

Thus one has the impression that the Diderotian *drame* has taken over images and feelings associated with Christian drama and enlisted them to a secular end. Like successive generations of Christian believers, participants in the reenactment of *Le Fils naturel* are meant to recognize their own mortality in the sacrifice of the Father, to cry over it, and to recognize in those tears intimations of their own immortality. Members of the next generation of subjects will also mortify themselves and eventually die, but their children will seek to take their place, and so on. Over the years, the accumulated cast of characters will always have been the same as the family tree, and each member of the family will have acted out his or her kinship with the departed Father, Lysimond. *Le Fils naturel*, or *The Genealogy of the Family.*

Virtue requires sacrifice, so much so that the entire effort at representation of the family's origin falls apart. As everyone finally realizes, the whole play breaks down in tears. Here is the final tableau:

> J'ai promis de dire pourquoi je n'entendis pas la dernière scène;
> et le voici. Lysimond n'était plus. On avait engagé un de ses
> amis, qui était à peu près de son âge, et qui avait sa taille,
> sa voix, et ses cheveux blancs, à le remplacer dans la pièce. Ce
> vieillard entra dans le salon, comme Lysimond y était entré
> la première fois, tenu sous les bras par Clairville et par André, et
> couvert des habits que son ami avait apportés des prisons.
> Mais à peine y parut-il que, ce moment de l'action remettant
> sous les yeux de toute la famille un homme qu'elle venait

de perdre, et qui lui avait été si respectable et si cher, personne ne put retenir ses larmes. Dorval pleurait, Constance et Clairville pleuraient. Rosalie étouffait ses sanglots et détournait ses regards. Le vieillard qui représentait Lysimond se troubla, et se mit à pleurer aussi. La douleur, passant des maîtres aux domestiques, devint générale, et la pièce ne finit pas.[11]

I promised to say why I did not hear the last scene; and here is why. Lysimond was no more. One of his friends had been engaged to replace him in the play, a man who was about Lysimond's age, and who had his stature, his voice, and his white hair. This old man entered the room, as Lysimond had entered the first time, held under the arms by Clairville and André, and covered with the same clothing which his friend had worn from prison. But hardly had he appeared when this moment of the action again placed before the eyes of the entire family a man they had just lost, and who had been so dear to them and worthy of respect, so that no one could hold back his tears. Dorval cried, Constance and Clairville cried, Rosalie suffocated her sobs and looked away. The old man who represented Lysimond became flustered, and began to cry, too. The pain, moving from the masters to the servants, became general, and the play was not completed.

Grief-stricken at this reminder of the father's recent death, the cast and the representation itself collapse in a paroxysm of collective tears. Doubtless the ritual of collective self-representation now makes their grief still more harrowing than it ever could have been a few days before the performance, when Lysimond "really" died. Because of the family emotional breakdown that was provoked by the entry of the friend (who is almost Lysimond, but not quite) who was to *play* the deceased father, the author of the play's preamble (*Moi*) did not see the last scene performed. Just as there was someone missing at the first performance of the play (namely, Lysimond the father), so there also was someone extra in attendance: the author of the preamble, Dorval's interlocutor in the *Entretiens*, the only person (aside from the servants) in attendance who was not a member of the family. It now becomes apparent that, just as Lysimond, father of the "natural son" (Dorval), has been the absent center of the play, so the "father" of the *Entretiens* has been watching from the wings all the time. Lysimond's structural counterpart, the "real" progenitor of Dorval and *Le Fils naturel*, the author wipes his eyes ("J'essuyais mes yeux") in exquisite anticipation of his own demise.

Analysis of the concluding tableau of *Le Fils naturel* thus reveals that the tableau not only provides a visible show, but also entails a representation of the beholder. Whether already constituted as an image (as in the plays) or simply providing material for an image (as in the narrative), Diderot's dialogic tableau always puts part of itself aside.

As representation, the tableau displays a loss in the family, but this loss is ideally recovered at the level of dialogue by the beholder. Indeed the tableau entails both the loss of the Father (origin, Author) and his ideal recovery by his children, while simultaneously recognizing that his recovery is only ideal (that no one will every satisfactorily occupy the position of the Father). Both the missing member and the one who plays his role are partial: that is, the missing part of the family and the actor/agent who plays his part are literally fragments, parts of a larger whole. But these are not quite the same parts, and not quite the same wholes. Neither quite fits. The author (the Father, the origin) had to be rejected, he had to be sacrificed (by his work, by his contemporaries), just as the beholder (or Son, who is also a "supplement") has to take his place. One misfit begets another.

Whatever its nominal genre (theater, narrative, art criticism, etc.), the tableau always casts off or sacrifices part of itself, a part that is to be captured and played by its future readers. The tableau always leaves that part to the imagination. This emphasis upon the theater of the imagination and the performance of the beholder rather than on the performance of actors on a stage doubtless corresponds to the declining importance of public space, in literature and elsewhere.[12] Even on the stage, the emphasis shifted from what is heard by an audience occupying a common space to what is "seen" in the mind's eye. In French Classical theater, only what is spoken *is*; but in the *drame*, of course, spoken language betrays its own inadequacy to convey what really matters. As Herbert Josephs has shown, gestures provided Diderot with a way of expressing the mobility of nature: "The flow of life in the universe, the vital forces contained within man, all this was expressed with immediacy in the dynamic and fugitive gesture that was born and that vanished with the rapidity of the pulsations of the mind."[13] In Diderot, no longer does speech define the real because truth is viewed as essentially unspoken, inaccessible to the conventions of speech. It is if only speech were culturally determined, framed by the interlocutors' situation, whereas gestures were a universal tongue, "la langue primitive de la nature." For Diderot, gesture is a discourse more authentic and natural than speech, unmediated by civilized constraints and hence closer to the flux of nature. Gesture addresses itself not to reason, but to the heart, and to the eye rather than to the ear.

What is meant to move the beholder in the spectacle of a Cleopatra, a Lysimond, or a Dorval are those things to which their words can only allude. When a tear or a sigh, an exclamation or ellipsis (. . .) interrupts their speech, the beholder bears witness to a struggle between natural forces and conventional speech. For example, Lysimond asks Dorval to record their family drama in the form of a play. What worlds of significance are evoked, but never revealed, in the son's elliptical answer: "Une pièce, mon père!" Four little words at once mention and omit, that is, *elide* the issues at stake for Dorval: the responsibilities of authorship and paternity; the genealogy of Dorval, the author, and the beholder. "A play, my father!" "(So you want me to write) a play, my father!" Or perhaps, "(Is) a play my father!" What these few words say cannot be compared with the portent of all they openly leave unsaid. Ellipsis is an indispensable figure in the rhetoric of pathos, for it is defined by what it omits. As befits Diderot, ellipsis is a paradoxical figure, too; for it labels its omissions as such. What Dorval's words purportedly omit, they in fact deliver to the imagination of the beholder. As with synecdoche, which enters into the dialogic structure of the tableau, the figure of ellipsis presents a part that stands in for a significantly absent whole. As with the fetish with which I have compared the tableau, ellipsis paradoxically includes at one level what it excludes at another; like the tableau, it invites the interlocutor to supply, with his imagination, the part of the message that has been sacrificed. Whether verbal or gestural, Diderot's language is dialogic.

As we have seen, the tableau places the beholder in the position of the Father. By playing the role of the tableau's absent origin (author, father), the beholder is meant to become its surrogate father—as if all participants in the tableau ("inside" and "outside" of it, as we shall see) were to form part of the same, finally happy family. For the father to reoccupy the position that is rightfully his, the beholder must shed a tear.

There is nothing specifically theatrical, of course, about this relationship between a representation and its beholder. It is true, as Szondi has argued, that the conflicts represented in the *drame* occur within the framework of private, middle-class existence, rather than in the public arena.[14] Yet this representation of private space, as we have seen, derives its pathetic force from a dialogic relationship (between the scene and its beholder) that itself is private, familial, and patriarchal. In fact, it would not be surprising if not only the *drames* but all of Diderot's texts bore these three dialogic marks, regardless of genre. Yet if Diderot's writing defines its interlocutor in terms of a private, patriarchal, family situation, it also creates a problem in the terms of the definition.

It is true that in Diderot everything happens *en famille*: that the world of social relations is modeled upon the domestic sphere, where the nuclear family mirrors the Family of Man. Whether on stage or off, both representations and the subjects who make representations —author, actors, beholder—never leave home, at least theoretically. But they are never quite at home either; they never quite fit into the representation. Whether Dorval or Suzanne Simonin, author or beholder, father or child, the subject is never where he or she belongs. The subject of the tableau is a loss in the family: part of the family, but not present to the family, never quite at home. Never entirely public (outside the family) or private (inside the family), this subject is located somewhere between private experience and conventional, public life. As we shall see in chapter 3, this subject is proper to "novelistic" experience.

In Diderot, this powerful tendency toward domestication or "familialization" of dialogic relations works even in those places that have nothing apparently "domestic" about them. In a letter to Sophie Volland dated 25 July 1762, Diderot tells a story whose hero is a king (not a *père de famille*) and that takes place in a public square. He tells of having met a Frenchman just returned from Copenhagen, where the man has witnessed an extraordinary scene, which "fera verser des larmes de joie dans deux cents ans, dans mille ans d'ici":

C'était à l'installation de la statue équestre du roi, sur une des places publiques de la capitale; le concours du peuple était immense. Le monarque était venu accompagné de toute sa cour. A peine avait-il paru, que voilà tout à coup deux à trois cent mille voix qui s'élèvent et qui crient à la fois: Vive notre roi! vive notre bon roi! vive notre maître, notre ami, notre père! et le souverain, partageant aussi tout à coup le transport de son peuple, d'ouvrir la portière de son carrosse, de s'élancer dans la foule, de jeter son chapeau en l'air, et de s'écrier: Vive mon peuple! vivent mes sujets! vivent mes amis! vivent mes enfants! et d'embrasser tous ceux qui se présentaient à lui. Ah! mon amie, que cela est rare et beau! l'idée de ce spectacle me fait tressaillir de joie, mon coeur en palpite, et je sens des larmes en tourner dans mes yeux. Ce récit nous a tous également attendris. Je relis cet endroit de ma lettre et il m'attendrit encore. Convenez que ce chapeau jeté en l'air marque une âme

bien enivrée. Quel est d'entre ses sujets le fortuné qui est
resté possesseur de ce chapeau? Si c'était moi, on m'en donnerait
sa forme toute pleine d'or que je n'échangerais pas. Quel
plaisir j'aurais de le montrer à mes enfants, mes enfants aux
leurs, et ainsi de suite jusqu'à ce que la famille s'éteignît!
Combien l'heureux moment qui m'en aurait rendu possesseur
se serait répété! combien je raconterais de fois avant que de
mourir! Croyez-vous que quelqu'on osât jamais le mettre sur sa
tête? Cet effet ne serait-il pas mille fois plus précieux que
l'épée de César Borgia, où l'on voit encore des gouttes de sang?
L'histoire de cette journée fera verser des larmes de joie
dans mille ans d'ici: qu'elle fut belle pour le monarque! qu'elle
fut belle pour ses sujets! Voilà le bonheur que j'envie aux
maîtres de la terre; causer l'ivresse d'un peuple immense, la voir,
la partager: c'est pour en mourir de plaisir. Au milieu de cette
allégresse publique, il fallait avoir perdu son père, ou avoir
été trahi de sa maîtresse pour être triste.[15]

It was at the installation of the equestrian statue of the king,
on one of the public squares of the capital; the people were
present in immense numbers. The monarch had come
accompanied by his entire court. He had scarcely appeared,
when lo and behold, two to three hundred thousand voices
suddenly rose up and together cried: Long live the king! Long
live our good king! Long live our master, our friend, our
father! And the sovereign, suddenly sharing his people's rapture,
opens the door of his carriage, throws himself into the crowd,
casts his hat in the air, and cries out: Long live my people! Long
live my subjects! and embraces all who appear before him.
Ah! My friend, how this is rare and beautiful! The idea of his
spectacle makes me flutter with joy, and I feel the tears coming
to my eyes. This story moved all of us equally. I reread this
part of my letter, and it moves me again. You will agree that
this hat tossed in the air is a sign of true exhilaration! Who
among his subjects is the fortunate one who retained possession
of this hat? If it were I, I would not trade that hat even for
its crown full of gold. What pleasure I would have in showing it
to my children, my children to theirs, and so on until the
family had died out! How often the happy moment which made
me its possessor would have been repeated! How many times
I would tell the tale before I died! Do you think that anyone
would ever dare put it on his head? Wouldn't this effect be
a thousand times more precious than the sword of Cesare Borgia,

where the drops of blood can still be seen? The story of this day
will cause tears of joy to be shed two hundred years, a thousand
years from now: how fine it was for the monarch! and how
fine for his subjects! This is the happiness for which I envy the
masters of the earth; to cause the elation of an immense crowd,
to see it, and share it: it's enough to die of pleasure. In the
midst of this public rejoicing, one would have to have lost one's
father, or have been betrayed by one's mistress in order to
be sad.

At the beginning of this scene, the beholder is drawn like the beholders represented in the scene to the installation of an equestrian
statue of the king on a public square in Copenhagen, in the presence
of the king himself. The statue, which Diderot elsewhere (cf. above,
chap. 1) imagines as a means of belated recognition for past greatness,
here monumentalizes for eternity a person who *actually is present*.
Apparently no one is missing; second, there is someone extra. Both
the living monarch and his deathless representation, two figures that
normally do not appear together, are both miraculously on the scene.
Normally a statue seems to occupy the same space that its living
model once occupied, but it can only do so because the model no
longer is present. Each figure, the statue and the organic model, each
usually implies the other's absence, but here are both at the same
time.

The statue's resemblance to its model is a strange one, especially in
Diderot's eyes. A statue tends to resemble its living, breathing model
in every way except that in principle it never changes: and change is
for Diderot the nature of life.[16] Just as the statue imitates its living
model, it also imitates previous statues of the same equestrian genre.
Yet the very existence of this artistic tradition again labels the statue
as only an idealized reproduction of its model. What makes this moment so special is that the models for all other equestrian statues in
the tradition have presumably passed away. The king (unlike his
statue) will continue to live—that is, to die—and the nearly simul-
taneous presence of the statue only serves, at a higher level, to make
the inevitable loss of the king that much more acutely felt.

For the assembled beholders, however, nothing disturbs the joy of
this scene; for them, the Father of the People is here, now and forever. In concentric circles, the people and assembled courtiers have
come to behold the king, himself the beholder of his immortal representation. Together, they are overwhelmed with delight, just as the
King's exuberant presence makes the scene *more than whole*. Not
only is no one missing from the scene, but this more than total

presence of a living family to itself ("Vive notre père!" . . . "Vivent mes enfants!") would be, Diderot suggests, more than one could bear. The king has only to appear in his carriage for the whole crowd to acclaim him, "two or three thousand voices" crying out at once. That gesture is answered in turn by the king, who responds to his "children" by opening the door of his coach, rushing into their arms, tossing his hat in the air, addressing their acclamations point by point with exclamations of his own, and, finally, embracing everyone who comes forward ("tous ceux *qui se présentaient à lui*"; my emphasis). The quickening rhythm of the parallel infinitive clauses underlines the rising intensity of the exchange. Each gesture in this dialogue, from the king's arrival to his final embraces of his subjects, is as if punctuated by an exclamation point. Each of these gestures translates, as it were, a spontaneous exuberance of being: first the king arrives, adding his presence to that of his statue; then the people are moved to express their emotion, and so on. With each gesture, another part is added to the scene, and another part is cast off from it (exclamations, emergence from the carriage, hat tossed in the air, more exclamations). With each gesture, the king and his subjects are "transported" with pleasure until the scene finally reaches what has to be called its climax ("C'est pour en mourir de plaisir").

Among the various parts that are played and cast off in this crescendo of dialogue, the part that most interests Diderot is that of the king, and especially the king's hat. The hat that the king tosses in the air, that he ejaculates, as it were, is the part that matters most for Diderot because this sacred hat has the power to engender nearly infinite representations of the scene in question. "Quel plaisir j'aurais de le montrer à mes enfants, mes enfants aux leurs. . . ." ["What pleasure I would have to show it to my children, my children to theirs. . . ."] After all, what really moves Diderot is not the scene itself, but someone else's account of it ("*Ce récit* nous a tous également attendris"; my emphasis) ["*This story* moved all of us equally"]. In fact, at the moment he writes to Sophie, he senses that it is the mere idea of this spectacle ("l'idée de ce spectacle") that makes him flutter with joy and cry. Moreover, that idea makes him feel so good that he rereads the part of the letter that he has just written, with the same results ("Je relis cet endroit de ma lettre et il m'attendrit encore"). Each time he reads the story, he places himself in the beholders's part, or better yet, in the part of the king. Each time he reads it, each time he quotes himself, his own unchanging discourse takes the place of a single, historical event; in the same way that the king's immutable statue replaces the king, the king's hat has the power to generate that story from generation to generation. Diderot has only to evoke its image to be able to move himself to tears.[17]

"Dangereux supplément," Rousseau might have added.[18] The need for infinite generations of beholders to bring the tableau to completion raised at least as many paradoxical questions for Diderot as the "supplemental" structure of representation did for Rousseau, but this infinite generation does not seem to have had anything sinful or "dangerous" about it. In contrast with Rousseau, who was concerned to construct a moment of absolute wholeness in the distant past, Diderot entrusts the achievement of that wholeness to the future anterior, to that moment when everything lacking in the present will have been made good.

The familial, patriarchal scene that Diderot ecstatically relates to Sophie is, of course, another tableau. The characters it represents are a father and his children, whose dialogic relationship engenders a beholder. When Diderot comes to play the beholder's part, he avers that, if only he possessed the single part—the hat—that has been lost, then he and his descendants could delight in it for as long as "the family" lasted. Yet he senses that a hat that this king has worn upon his head will never quite fit the profane head of a middle-class family. If only the philosophe had that sacred hat, he and his descendants could come together and behold this tableau in which the Father of the People and his descendants are joined in rapture: Voilà le bonheur que j'envie aux maîtres de la terre; causer l'ivresse d'un peuple immense, la voir, la partager. . . ." ["This is the happiness for which I envy the masters of the earth; to cause the elation of an immense crowd, to see it, and share it. . . ."] Both Diderot and the king whose happiness he envies would then appear simultaneously at the center of the picture ("au milieu de cette allégresse publique") and outside it. Authors of the family's rapture as well as its beholders ("causer l'ivresse . . . , la voir"), they would be outside the tableau, while in it ("la partager") at the same time. If Diderot could manage to play the king's part, he would be a "fortunate subject" indeed because he would have the fortune of participating in the generation of beholders and in the spectacle itself, while at the same time retaining recognition as their (that is, his own) author. If he really possessed the king's magic hat, he would have the fortune of transcending his own subjectivity—of *really* "dying of pleasure." Unless, the passage concludes, unless *his own father* had just died, or he had just lost his mistress.

The king's hat has a political meaning, too. It signifies the difference between despotism and enlightened despotism, between the bloody sword of that "Machiavellian" prince, Cesare Borgia, and the Danish monarch, who cares for his subjects with a father's love. Perhaps of even greater political significance, however, in the complex organization of Diderot's *tableau généalogique*, is the apparently minor role that women, mothers and daughters, play in the dialogue. They seem to appear only at the level of represented characters (suffering widows, et al.), whereas the author and the beholder are always men. In the following chapters, I shall investigate the literary and political meaning of this situation through a reading of dialogue in *La Religieuse*.

Chapter Three
Moving Pictures (*La Religieuse*—I)

Literary history has revealed that *La Religieuse* was the product of "a horrible plot."[1] In late 1759, we know that Grimm, Diderot, and others set out to recall their friend, the Marquis de Croismare, from his Norman meditations by means of a "mystification." By soliciting the marquis's sympathy for the plight of a fictional nun, they hoped to lure their friend back to Paris. At some point after the initial exchange of letters between the nun and the marquis, Diderot assumed sole authorship of the nun's letters. He expanded and rewrote them until as late as 1781 or 1782, for a total of at least 22 years, and until long after the Marquis de Croismare had abandoned whatever belief he may have had in the real existence of the poor Suzanne Simonin.[2] Scholars disagree over the extent to which the marquis may have taken this fiction for reality.[3] Whatever the case may be, if Diderot began as a willing participant in a friendly joke, he ended up by taking his own creation not only seriously, but quite out of the hands of his collaborators.

If the marquis was indeed duped into taking the perils of Suzanne for a true story, it was not the first time that the tenuous distinction between the referential and literary values of discourse had become a worrisome topic in our culture. In the Classical Age, not only had Cervantes' fictional Don Quixote been subject to this confusion, but even "real" people, aristocrats in fact, had caused some concern by behaving as if reality were a chivalric romance:

In gallant circles, one took names borrowed from heroes of romances. Tallemant, among his friends, was called the Knight because he was mad about the *Amadis*, and his relatives were called Lysis, or Ligdamon, or Tirsis.[4]

But if the possibility of mistaking what the modern world calls "literature" for discourse about the real world has always been inherent in language, it is characteristic of the Classical Age that this potential confusion should have become a social problem.

In *Histoire de la folie à l'âge classique*, Michel Foucault described some of the centralizing discursive strategies that the Classical Age devised to regulate unreasonable behavior (of which quixotism was a recognized variant).[5] Starting from a reading of prefaces to early English and French novels, Gianni Celati has also been able to show that the rise of the novel testifies to the emergence in Western discourse of individual, bodily experience ("empirical singularity"), on the one hand; and of a strategy, "fiction," for regulating that experience.[6] Fictions, Celati contended, function as a sort of social hygiene, regulating the historically new realm of the individual body, of "private experience," by labeling it as only a reasonable fasimile (*finzione*) of experience. These early prefaces emphasize that novels address themselves only to "mature" readers—people with their heads on their shoulders, so to speak—to persons of "understanding" who don't need to be reminded that "It's only a story." The novel allows such readers to penetrate into the experience of a Moll Flanders, for example, but only after that experience has been processed into socially acceptable form or "common language":

> If everyone has this common ground on which to communicate,
> . . . this keeps the local singularities of a story, a passion
> or an extraordinary vice from turning into personal phantasms,
> from obsessing someone as chivalric stories had obsessed
> Don Quixote.[7]

As a discursive strategy, the novel allows individual bodies to communicate with each other; it reveals and sometimes even *moves* these bodies, but it also tries to keep them at a reasonable distance from each other.

This strategy is true at least in theory, at least according to the supposedly detached vision posited in the prefaces of these early novels, according to which the reader distances himself from whatever the body of the novel may enable him to experience. By saying "distance *him*self," I do not mean to suggest, contrary to available evidence, that early novels addressed themselves primarily to men, but rather to underline the socially determined "masculine" capacity for detachment (from representations, feelings, etc.) to which these fictions appealed, and which they reinforced in their readers. Later in this chapter, I shall say more about this question of rhetorical sex and class position.

Of course, the experience of readers of fiction has always belied this appeal to "masculine" detachment. "Mature readers" of both sexes and all classes have been known to identify themselves with what they "knew" to be only fictive constructs. The case of Diderot and *La Religieuse* is an example. According to the 1770 preface, attributed by Diderot to Grimm, the collective authors of Suzanne Simonin had started off by laughing at the products of their "mystification," these letters that were meant to make the marquis cry:

> Nous passions alors nos soupers à lire, au milieu des éclats de rire, des lettres qui devaient faire pleurer notre bon marquis, et nous y lisions avec ces mêmes éclats de rire les réponses honnêtes que ce digne et généreux ami lui faisait.[8]

> At that time we spent our suppers, amid peals of laughter, reading the letters which were to make our good marquis cry, and it was amid the same peals of laughter that we would read the honest answers which this worthy and generous friend made her.

Nonetheless, we are told, as Diderot continued to develop this fiction, his laughter turned to tears. Soon he supposedly found himself so caught up in the story of this fictional nun that, not only expanding the autobiographical passages of her letters to book length, he would even cry at the sufferings of his own creation:

> Un jour qu'il était tout entier à ce travail, M. d'Alainville, un de nos amis communs, lui rendit visite, et le trouva plongé dans la douleur et le visage inondé de larmes. "Qu'avez-vous donc," lui dit M. d'Alainville? "Comme vous voilà!" "Ce que j'ai?" lui répondit M. Diderot; "*je me désole d'un conte que je fais.*" . . .[9] [My emphasis]

> One day when he was completely engrossed in this work, Mr. D'Alainville, one of our common friends, paid him a visit, and found him plunged in distress and his face flooded with tears. "What is wrong with you?" Mr. D'Alainville said to him. "What a state you're in!" "What is wrong with me?" Mr. Diderot answered him; "*I'm upset over a tale that I'm making.*" . . .)

Whether or not this anecdote from the preface is true, it raises questions of poetics that are part and parcel of the novel itself. In the preface, the author supposedly manages to affect himself through the mediation of his fictional progeny; he moves his own body, first to laughter, and then to tears. In the body of the novel, all of Suzanne's rhetorical efforts are bent upon eliminating the separation between her paternal reader and herself, at ensuring that her pathetic story makes him cry with her, and not laugh at her. Yet she must claim to do so, without ever moving herself.

If it was by taking a distance from the fictional nun and her apparently nonfictional correspondent that Diderot and his friends were able to laugh (at Croismare), was it through "identification" with the fictional body of the nun that her author or her reader could be made to cry? And if he could identify with "her" body, to what extent is "his" body his own? Doubtless all novelistic fictions play upon the ambiguity between the literary and referential values of discourse; all fictions ask their readers to believe in a facsimile of reality, but *La Religieuse* raises this typical characteristic of fiction to the level of a strategy.

Critics have noted the many inconsistencies in the novel's point of view: indeed, from its very first sentence,[10] Diderot's novel shuttles between third-person and first-person narration, between a story told *about* Suzanne Simonin and a story told *by* her. Yet rather than interpret these inconsistencies as only errors in performance, mistakes that Diderot could have corrected but somehow (while rewriting the manuscript) never managed to smooth out, one may also view them as integral parts of the performance, deliberate or not. These inconsistencies may also be seen as ways in which Diderot's text becomes problematic by placing its own identity (and that of its author and reader) in question. I have already pointed to several problematic aspects of *La Religieuse*, each of which raises a question of identity: Is this fiction or nonfiction? Which is its point of view? Will the reader laugh or cry? And whose body will be moved? Each of these questions arises from the tendency in Diderot's novel for mutually exclusive categories (fiction and nonfiction, first- and third-person narration, laughter and tears) to generate and to include each other.

In previous chapters, I observed this process of self-questioning in the Diderotian tableau, which I described as a kind of dialogue whose characters or parts (author, characters, beholder) require, exclude, and produce each other. Here I shall argue that the dialogic structure of the tableau is duplicated, on a larger scale, by the dialogic structure of *La Religieuse* as a novel. *La Religieuse* also makes the dialogic relationships that produce it problematic by never quite establishing whether its author, heroine, and reader are inside or outside of the novel. Reading the book, one is never quite sure whether one is meant to stand at a distance from the characters and appreciate how artfully their narration has been constructed, or whether one is to be moved by Suzanne's perils; one does not know whether this story calls for laughter or for tears. Never does a clear distinction emerge between the topic of this fiction ("The Nun") and the agents (author, reader) whose dialogue with the fiction produces both them and it; in other words, there is never a neat distinction between the two senses (topic, agent) in which one speaks of a novel's subject. Apparently, both author and reader wish to keep their distance from this pathetic fiction, but each tends to identify with it (with *her*). Hence one cannot decide, once and for all, whether the subject of that fiction is inside or outside of the body of the novel, inside or outside of the bodies of Diderot, Suzanne, and the reader. As was the case for the tableau, none of the constituent parts ever quite fits with the others.

In *La Religieuse*, tableaux are charged with such intensity that they seem to motivate, rather than to stop the narrative. It is as if the narrative component of the text served mainly to prepare the way for these "moving pictures," as if the action had the paradoxical function of enabling these moving instants when all movement comes to a halt and meaning overflows. With each tableau, Suzanne presents her interlocutors with one of the trials that she has undergone in the hope that he will be moved to free her from the convent. These tableaux mark the most pathetic places in the autobiographical testimony that she gives before her judge.[11] The trials that tableaux convey are thus part of the much longer trial (or Passion) that constitutes her narration. Like the images that invited the Christian to shed tears before various stations of the Savior's Passion, the tableaux of *La Religieuse* call upon the reader to be moved by the tears and suffering of an innocent victim, and to be moved from tears to action.[12] With each tableau, the reader is presented with a striking vision. Each time, it is as if Suzanne were saying, "Voilà!" [literally, "Look here!"] "Behold, and see my trials." In classical rhetoric, this figure was called *hypotyposis*.[13]

At the origin of the narrative, just such a vision moves Suzanne to write. She tells the marquis that seeing a tableau made her vow to refuse convent life:

Il est sûr, monsieur, que sur cent religieuses qui meurent avant cinquante ans, il y en a cent tout juste de damnées, sans compter celles qui deviennent folles, stupides ou furieuses en attendant.

Il arriva un jour qu'il s'en échappa une de ces dernières de la cellule où on la tenait renfermée. *Je la vis.* Voilà l'époque de mon bonheur ou de mon malheur, selon, monsieur, la manière dont vous en userez avec moi. Je n'ai jamais rien vu de si hideux. Elle était *échevelée* et presque sans vêtement; elle traînait des chaînes de fer; ses yeux étaient égarés; elle s'arrachait les cheveux; elle se frappait la poitrine avec les poings, elle courait, elle hurlait; elle se chargeait elle-même, et les autres, des plus terribles imprécations; elle cherchait une fenêtre pour se précipiter. La frayeur me saisit, je tremblai de tous mes membres, je vis mon sort dans celui de cette infortunée, et sur-le-champ il fut décidé, dans mon coeur, que je mourrais mille fois plutôt que de m'y exposer.[14] [My emphasis]

It is a certain fact, Sir, that out of every hundred nuns who die before fifty there are exactly one hundred damned, and that taking no account of the ones who in the meantime lose their reason, get feeble-minded or go raving mad.

There came a day when one of these last escaped from the cell where she was shut up. *I saw her.* That was the beginning of my good or bad fortune – according, Sir, to how you treat me henceforth. I have never seen anything so horrible. She was all *disheveled* and half naked, she was dragging iron chains, wild-eyed, tearing her hair and beating her breast, rushing along and shrieking. She was heaping upon herself and everyone else the most appalling curses, and looking for a window to throw herself out of. I was seized with panic and trembled in every limb, seeing my own fate in that of this unhappy creature, and thereupon a vow was made in my heart that I would die a thousand deaths rather than expose myself to it.

Three words, "Je la vis," three syllables set this tableau apart from the rest of the story. The three words posit the minimal terms of a hypotyposis. That the subject ("je") should encounter the object ("la") in this way, through vision ("vis"), betrays the scopic drive behind the tableau. It is as if the most "striking" object were that which, by virtue of visual distance, could only "strike" the viewing subject figuratively. The tableau can move the spectator to identify with what she (e.g. Suzanne) or he (e.g. the marquis) sees, thanks to the preliminary distance (absence) that sight implies. Like the candles and torches that cast light upon the action elsewhere in this story, the past definite tense of *voir* isolates and frames the spectacle about to follow, defining it (and hence its spectator) against the darker backdrop of the framing narration.

Just as a tableau that she witnessed impelled Suzanne to write her story, it may very well be that Diderot was moved to write *La Religieuse* by a remembered image of his own sister's fate.[15] Whatever the case, there has never been any serious doubt that a polemical intention directs the pathetic tableaux that compose *La Religieuse*, that these tears have a political significance. Already the preface had underscored the sociopolitical import of all this pathos:

> On n'en pouvait pas lire une page sans verser des pleurs; et
> cependant il n'y avait point d'amour; ouvrage de génie
> qui présentait partout la plus forte empreinte de l'imagination
> de l'auteur; ouvrage d'une utilité publique et générale, car
> c'était la plus cruelle satire qu'on eût jamais faite des cloîtres.[16]

> One could not read a page of it without shedding tears; and yet
> there was no love story; a work of genius which everywhere
> bears the most powerful imprint of the author's imagination; a
> work of public and general utility, for it was the cruelest
> satire of cloisters which had ever been written.

Apparently less of a love story than an attack upon the institution of female celibacy, the novel still compelled this reader (who probably was also the writer) to tears. Unlike Richardson's *Clarissa*, the central conflict here is not between a suffering heroine and a powerful man, but between the heroine and a powerful institution. Lovelace wants to possess Clarissa's body sexually, while the various representatives of Suzanne's institutional antagonist wish to dispossess her of the liberty to dispose of "her body" as she chooses. How then does this latter conflict between the body of a nun and a Religious Body come to move first Diderot, and then subsequent readers, to tears? Surely the pathetic force of Suzanne's story derives from the way in which it incorporates and plays upon the body. When the mother superior of Suzanne's third convent asks her to tell the story of her sufferings, the bodily erotic component of narrative pathos is made explicit:

> "Mais," lui dis-je, "chère Mère, cela sera bien long et bien
> triste, et je ne voudrais pas vous attrister si longtemps." "Ne
> crains rien, j'aime à pleurer, c'est un état délicieux pour
> une âme tendre que celui de verser des larmes. Tu dois aimer à
> pleurer aussi, tu essuierais mes larmes, j'essuierai les tiennes,

et peut-être nous serons heureuses au milieu du récit de tes
souffrances; qui sait jusqu'où l'attendrissement peut nous
mener?"[17]

"But, dear Mother, it will be very long and very depressing,
and I don't want to make you miserable for so long."

"Don't be afraid, I love a good cry, and to be shedding tears
is a delicious state for a sensitive soul. You must enjoy weeping
too—you will wipe away my tears and I yours, and perhaps
we shall be happy in the middle of the tale of your sufferings,
and who knows where our emotion may lead us?"

Even when the listener-reader of Suzanne's tale is not represented
(as in the previous example) by a character in the story, Suzanne's
suffering body remains charged with erotic interest.[18] For example,
just prior to the famous night scene, during which Suzanne is made
to suffer in her secular body, when she must once again undergo a
ritual ascesis before being reincorporated into the Religious Body
from which she has been symbolically expelled:

J'avais la tête nue, les pieds nus, mes longs cheveux tombaient
sur mes épaules, et tout mon vêtement se réduisait à ce cilice
que l'on me donna, à une chemise très dure, et à cette longue
robe qui me prenait sous le cou et qui me descendait jusqu'aux
pieds.[19]

My head was uncovered and I was barefoot, my long hair fell
over my shoulders, and my whole clothing consisted only
of this hair shirt I had been given, a very coarse chemise and the
long garment which came up to my neck and reached down
to my feet.

It is a mildly sadistic representation with which the author moves
himself here—rough fabric inflicting punishment upon young flesh—
but doubtless also characteristic of the way in which eroticized pathos
works throughout the novel. Reading this portrait, the reader touches
Suzanne through the vicarious agency of the symbol, and he himself
is "touched."

The tableau of eroticized pathos enables author and reader each to
be moved, a possibility ostensibly denied to the innocent narrator,
and doubtless also moves him to identify with his own (re)creation.
As Jauss has argued, this process of identification is a constantly
shifting one, whereby an empirical subject moves in and out of various rhetorical positions:

In the course of reception, the spectator or reader passes
through a sequence of attitudes. Astonishment, admiration,
being shaken or touched, sympathetic tears and laughter,
or estrangement constitute the scale of such primary levels of
aesthetic experience which the performance or the reading
of a text brings with it.[20]

In the case of the pathetic tableau, this subject (or beholder) may
momentarily occupy either a represented role (hero or heroine) or
the role of beholder (often, but not always represented in the text),
in which cases (s)he may cry; or (s)he may take a distance from these
roles, and laugh. Whether the outcome is tears or laughter, the reader will have been moved, that is, both touched and displaced from
one rhetorical position to another.

To describe the theoretical implications of the dialogic effects
that are produced by the act of reading, I have found myself invent-
ing several cumbersome or unavoidably vague expressions, such as
"rhetorical positions" or "a certain body." To account for these
dialogic effects in the area of aesthetics requires one to think of
pleasure in social terms, in terms of socially determined interactions
between individuals and discourse. For Bakhtin, neither stylistics nor
linguistics takes into account the thoroughly social character of language. He attempted to bridge the gap between conceiving of language
in too narrowly individualistic terms (as in stylistics) or in terms too
general (as in linguistics) by positing the notion of *utterance type*:

In language, there is no word or form left that would be neutral
or would belong to no one: all of language turns out to be
scattered, permeated with intentions, accented. For the
consciousness that lives in it, language is not an abstract system
of normative forms but a concrete heterological opinion on
the world. Every word gives off the scent of a profession,
a genre, a current, a party, a particular work, a particular man, a
generation, an era, a day, and an hour.[21]

Transposing Bakhtin's argument into the area of aesthetic experience,
I have been supposing throughout this text that aesthetic experience
is not only socially determined but dialogic, that it entails discursive
interaction. Aesthetic "response" is a dialogic (and not only a biological) gesture; as such, laughter or tears (for example) address
themselves both to previous discourses about the same topic and to
the anticipated responses of an interlocutor. Not only discourse, but

the body itself is social as well as socially determined: in other words, one's body is always to some extent, a *typical* or generic body.

From this perspective, then, I would argue for the necessity of distinguishing between the social position of the emergent novel's audience and the rhetorical positions that it made available to that "new reading public";[22] and, moreover, that these positions should be understood in terms of typical (or generic) pleasures. In the case of the novel, my contention is that the pleasure of "beholding" a tableau is emblematic of the generic pleasure of reading a novel. The tableau, I suggested above, is basically a figure of dramatic revelation (hypotyposis), just as the novel (as Celati argued) is a genre of dramatic revelation that allows the reader to penetrate into private experience within one's own society.[23] Obviously, to speak of "revelation" and "penetration" implies the (rhetorical) gender position that the reader of a novelistic fiction is asked to occupy. Reading *La Religieuse* also suggests that this "phallic" position, the position of the missing part, is only the first rhetorical position that the genre posits, for the full range of novelistic pleasure requires that the reader also enjoy the complementary "feminine" pleasure of "identifying" with the intensity of this private experience.

The emergence of the novel doubtless betokens not only changing class relationships, but also a reorganization of sexual markers within the society as a whole. The novel at once reemphasizes the "feminine" pleasure of identifying with others and seeks to subordinate that pleasure to the "masculine" pleasure of maintaining a critical detachment. Sensing himself unjustly subservient to the cold and "virile" nobleman, the bourgeois found in the novel a means to assert the ethical superiority of his identification with private experience; simultaneously, he could label that identification as only imaginary, as *fiction*. By demonstrating a capacity for both tears and laughter, the bourgeois could contrast the warmth of ideal family life with the heartlessness of the public, economic world and could designate that very capacity as the virtue that entitled him to rule over both the private and the public spheres.

If the novel revalorizes both empirical singularity and rational abstraction—the body and the head, experience and theory—*La Religieuse* plays upon these categories and places them in question. Because of various "inconsistencies" in the novel's style, one is urged to hesitate between laughing and crying, between identifying with Suzanne Simonin and viewing her trials from a distance. Whatever the aesthetic response, the reader (he or she) can nonetheless hope (like Suzanne's third mother superior) that "peut-être nous serons heureuses au milieu du récit de tes souffrances; qui sait jusqu'où l'attendrissement peut nous mener?"

These rhetorical positions, like those of any figure, entail varying proportions of pleasure and displeasure. However much the reader or the author may enjoy "feeling feminine" or making someone else feel that way, she or he is defined by the novel in relation to these positions. Of course, it was the sadistic and masochistic elements of sentimental representation that led us to develop the notion of rhetorical position: in the sentimental novel, "feeling feminine" or "making someone feel feminine" requires suffering (Passion). By alternately occupying the roles of "female" victim and "male" reader, one's body might indeed be moved in this fashion. Moreover, it now appears that Suzanne's passionate (that is, suffering) body mediates here between the bodies of an author and a reader who are both "men." In this sentimental novel, as well as in Sade later on, the fundamental narrative bond is between virile figures (regardless of their gender): a "man" is invited to share with a member of his own rhetorical gender in the pleasure of making a female figure suffer and of occasionally suffering with her.

A pathetic and erotic bond here again links dialogic figures in a common, paternal position. The Marquis de Croismare, nominal interlocutor of the tale, is said to have a daughter of Suzanne's age, and so does Diderot.[24] As with the tableaux that paradoxically motivate and arrest this novel, narrative relations in *La Religieuse* are familial. Inside and outside of the convents, Suzanne stands between a series of mother and father figures—from her mother and (legal) father to several mother superiors and paternal clergymen (Grand Vicar Hébert, Lemoyne)—as well as among a complement of biological and contractual "sisters."

Whereas her original family relationships are not happy ones, they are at least partially based upon love and blood; but family relations in the convent are mediated solely by contractual obligations: the size of her dowry determines a nun's relationship to her mother and sisters. In this figurative family, however attached specific individuals may become to each other, the existence of the Family does not depend on them as individuals. Mothers and sisters come and go, as do readers of *La Religieuse*, but the figurative family (like the novel) has a transcendent, institutional reality.

Of course, what Suzanne hopes to discover outside of the convent is the happiness of family relationships such as she (or doubtless her reader) has never known them: a family in which the contradictions between love and money, between the intensity of experience and social order, would somehow have been overcome. Instead of this happiness, at the end of her quest Suzanne had found only a choice among various ways of selling her body: marriage, prostitution, or wage labor. Once she escapes from the convent, the only semblance of a mother she can find is her employer in a laundry, and the paternal Croismare's answer comes too late to save her from death. *Fille naturelle*, she does not fit into any form of this social order. On the other hand, while her story appeals to a loving father, her actual readers do not need to fulfill that requirement: the abstract power of money is quite enough for anyone to buy the book and offer herself or himself the pleasure of either laughing at or crying with poor Suzanne.

Something about her "nature" not only moves her author and reader, but destines Suzanne for expulsion from the various family units in which she is placed. Something about her nature and theirs — call it an *air de famille* — makes it impossible for any of the participants in this dialogue to fit into any of the places that a novel conventionally assigns to them. Like Dorval, Suzanne is a "natural" child, a *fille naturelle*; like him, she is naturally asocial. Other, mythical features of her nature overdetermine this exclusion: she is the youngest of three sisters, innocent and yet (like Cordelia or Cinderella) persecuted and cut off from her family, repudiated by her parents; or, like the hero of the most famous Passion story, she is conceived not by her legal father but by a mysterious figure, only to be cast out into the world to be sacrificed by the agents of an unjust and corrupt society.

Her "naturalness" poses difficult rhetorical problems, too. As narrator, she must appear innocent to move her judge, but the very existence of her mimetic narration (whose sadistic component I have already noted) testifies to an experience that is incompatible with virginal innocence. Although this story is a product of Enlightenment rhetoric, it makes knowledge or enlightenment about certain matters tantamount to sin: Suzanne's confessor says as much when he warns her against "des lumières funestes que vous ne pourriez acquérir sans vous perdre"[25] [poisonous knowledge which you couldn't acquire without loss]. Suzanne's narrative must always supply enough information for the reader to understand what is happening and to be moved by it, yet the purport of the narration itself must remain unintelligible to her: as if she could understand only isolated moments in that narration, but not the relations among them; as if she understood individual utterances, but were quite incapable of grasping the narrative syntax.

To be moved by the story, the reader and author must know how to affect themselves, how to touch their own bodies, albeit symbolically; at the same time, they will not be moved unless that capacity is apparently denied to the heroine, their symbolic daughter. Suzanne's rhetorical effectiveness depends upon her appearing innocent, not only of sex, but of auto-affection. Her superior asks her:

> "Jamais vous n'avez pensé à promener vos mains sur cette gorge, sur ces cuisses, sur ce ventre, sur ces chairs si fermes si douces et si blanches?" "Oh, pour cela, non, il y a du péché à cela, et si cela m'était arrivé, je ne sais comment j'aurais fait pour l'avouer à confession." . . .[26]

> "It has never occurred to you to run your hands over that lovely bosom, those legs, that body, that firm, soft, white flesh of yours?"
> "Oh no, that is sinful, and if such a thing had happened to me I don't know how I could ever have mentioned it in my confession. . . ."

Again, since her "nature" is exactly what must be punished in order for her judges to find her appealing, she must appear natural, represent herself as natural, but ostensibly never to herself.

This novel has the form of a message addressed by one father to another about their symbolic (and hence, absent) daughter. Her symbolic presence places them in communication. We have already suggested reasons for understanding the tableau and the *drame* as a paternal (as well as paternalistic) discourse, whose main character, author, and beholder are each a *père de famille*. This same dialogic model organizes *La Religieuse* as a discourse addressed by one Family Man to another. In both these discourses, "men" (fathers, in fact) are made to communicate with each other through their symbolic female progeny. I am not sure whether it is more important to emphasize the incestuous character of the father-daughter relationship here or the homosexual character of the discursive situation. Although the young daughter's body is presented as the visible center of dramatic and erotic interest, the gender represented here may matter less than the gender of those making the representation.

Diderot's novel expresses a search for human relationships that, ideally, would not be vitiated by money and by the unjust exercise of power. The model for such an arrangement is the family, where a benevolent father oversees the welfare of all concerned. One may wish to see this figure as analogous to that of an "enlightened" monarch, as in Diderot's image of the king of Denmark as "father of the people." A conception of family relationships as the very model of human authenticity is contradicted throughout the novel by the heroine's actual experience, just as Diderot's explicit desire for the wholeness of conversation (*parole pleine*) may have been frustrated by his own experience as a writer who had to address an unknown and anonymous audience. For both heroine and author, there is a contradiction between desire and experience, and yet no synthetic term to mediate between the two. As in the image (in *Le Neveu de Rameau* or the Falconet correspondence) of the unrecognized genius who will only be recognized after his death by the erection of a statue, *La Religieuse* presents true happiness and successful communication as things that can be had only at the price of one's life. A stern but loving father willing to authorize the desires of a *fille naturelle* was not to be found in this world. No term mediates the contradiction, just as no one ever quite fits into the paternal role that the novel calls for so poignantly.

Another level of unmediated contradiction in *La Religieuse* can be observed in the relationship between the empirical singularity of a body and the abstraction from that singularity upon which institutions such as the convent and the novel are based, between the individual body and what I have called the "typical" or "generic" body. If the novel as a genre both opens up and domesticates the realm of free bodily intensities, the story of Suzanne Simonin has critical implications that go far beyond its explicit attack upon convents. I shall develop some of these implications in the next chapter. Perhaps the convent exemplifies a whole set of institutions, both pre- and post-Revolutionary, which *as institutions must abstract* from free bodily instensities. Yet if pre-Revolutionary institutions simply did not recognize these intensities, post-Revolutionary institutions both recognize them and set out to regulate them. In this period of transition from one order to another, the institution of novelistic discourse (like that of the nuclear family) worked in both directions: both as a vehicle for domestication of experience and as a way of revealing to each individual the terrifying possibilities of life, of what Georges Bataille (in the "Avant-Propos" to *Le Bleu du Ciel*) called the "multiple truth" of life:

Un peu plus, un peu moins, tout homme est suspendu aux *récits*, aux *romans*, qui leur révèlent la vérité multiple de la vie. Seuls ces récits, lus parfois dans les transes, le situent devant le destin. . . . Comment nous attarder à des livres auxquels, sensiblement, l'auteur n'a pas été contraint? [Bataille's emphasis[27]

> A little more, a little less, every man is suspended from the
> *stories*, from the *novels* which reveal to them the multiple truth
> of life. Only these stories, read sometimes in trances, place
> him in front of his destiny. . . . How can we linger over books
> which the author was manifestly not compelled to write?

Whether or not *La Religieuse* does succeed in moving its reader to
tears or laughter, its author was clearly compelled to write it. He was
compelled to do so by an acute sense of the irresolvable contradiction between the free bodily intensities that certain stories tend to
reveal and the tendency of these same stories, as *fictions* in Celati's
sense, to limit these intensities.

   La Religieuse, like the novel as a genre, both releases the body and
regulates it, gives rein to passion and sublimates it. *La Religieuse* carries out this contradictory function by at once calling for the liberation of the body from various forms of generic constraint and by
subjecting the body (of the character, author, and reader) to narrative relations that are themselves generic, those of the family.

Chapter Four
Misfits (*La Religieuse*—II)

I have suggested that *La Religieuse* could be viewed in terms of a contradiction in Diderot between empirical singularity and generic abstraction; between the demands of the heroine's "natural" body and the necessity for institutions (such as the convent, the family, and the novel) to abstract from that body, to "civilize" it. There is a long and justly famous speech in *La Religieuse* that contains a indictment of convents and monasteries, a passage that imposes itself as *the* place where Diderot's opinion of convents is expressed. This passage exemplifies the sort of contradiction of which I have been speaking.

One cannot easily attribute this speech to any single speaker. It begins as a first-person narration by Suzanne, who criticizes certain excesses of convent life, but without placing the institution itself in fundamental question: religious celibacy should be voluntary, not forced, she says; human lives are needlessly wasted in convents; and the proof of true Christianity lies in charitable acts, rather than in prayer. The speech concludes, however, as the discourse of Suzanne's lawyer, Manouri ("'On ne sait pas l'histoire de ces asiles,' disait ensuite M. Manouri dans son plaidoyer"), whose final words are: "La vie claustrale est d'un fanatique ou d'un hypocrite."[1] ["'Nobody knows the story of these places,' went on Monsieur Manouri in his argument. . . . The cloistered life is that of a fanatic or a hypocrite.'"

It is precisely this apparent slip in point of view that gives one the impression that Diderot has allowed himself to get so carried away by his subject (and therefore so detached from his heroine) that he has forgotten to make the perspective of the whole passage consistent. This change in point of view occurs when, in a long series of rhetorical questions, the speaker goes beyond Suzanne's moderate criticisms to contest the very existence of convents and monsteries. These, we are told, are fundamentally *unnatural* institutions: it is not in nature, it is not in human nature to live in such places; only unnatural creatures, "monsters," can thrive in them:

> Ces voeux, qui heurtent la pente générale de la nature, peuvent-ils jamais être bien observés que par quelques créatures mal organisées, en qui les germes des passions sont flétris, et qu'on rangerait à bon droit parmi les *monstres* . . . ? Toutes ces cérémonies lugubres qu'on observe à la prise d'habit et à la profession, quand on consacre un homme ou une femme à la vie monastique et au malheur, suspendent-elles les fonctions animales?[2] [My emphasis]

> Can *these vows, which run counter to our natural inclinations*, ever be properly observed except by a few abnormal creatures in whom the seeds of passion are dried up, and whom we should rightly classify as *freaks of nature* . . . ? Do all these lugubrious ceremonies played out at the taking of the habit or the profession, when a man or woman is set apart for the monastic life and for woe, suspend the animal functions?

If the sensuous demands of the body are repressed or ignored, the speaker says, they will nonetheless make themselves known: either the "natural" human economy will break down, when

> la nature révoltée d'une contrainte pour laquelle elle n'est point faite, brise les obstacles qu'on lui oppose, devient furieuse, jette l'économie animale dans un désordre auquel il n'y a plus de remède. . . .[3]

> nature, outraged at constraint for which she is not designed, breaks down the obstacles put in her way and in a frenzy of madness throws the working of our bodies into a disorganization beyond all curing?

or the walls of the convent will be broken down by a revolutionary mob (*foule*):

> L'homme politique . . . sent secrètement que, si l'on

souffrait que les portes de ces prisons s'abattissent en faveur
d'une malheureuse, la foule s'y porterait et chercherait à
les forcer.[4]

The politician . . . feels in his heart of hearts that if the prison
gates were once allowed to be thrown down in favour of one
unhappy woman, the whole mob would hurl itself against them
and try to force them.

Now there is no reason to believe that this passage does not express Diderot's deeply held convictions. Indeed, other Diderot texts
(such as the *Supplément au Voyage de Bougainville*)[5] carry the argument from human nature to even more radical conclusions. Yet in all
of these texts, the argument based upon "natural" desires and
changeability is only part of the story. Invariably, Diderot's assertions of the essential changeability of nature and human nature are
countered by more conservative positions, as in the passage just cited.

Besides, the philosophe's indictment of convents as unnatural
institutions is paradoxical at least, coming as it does in the middle of
a novel whose dialogic relations thematize the generic necessity of
policing as well as releasing the body. Suzanne's story is meant to affect her reader's body, but here the liberation of affect is not simply
an end in itself. The pleasure of discovering what nobody knows
("On ne sait pas l'histoire de ces asiles") ["Nobody knows the story
of these places"] is meant to have a point. What "nobody knows"
(that is, what Celati argued that novels are about) is meant here to
produce specific action (whether erotic or political, or both). As
Suzanne's third mother superior puts it, "Qui sait jusqu'où l'attendrissement peut nous mener?"

Just as Suzanne was moved to undertake her liberation by the tableau of a mad nun, so the further meaning of her story (insofar as it
has any) will have been determined by the effect that this and subsequent tableaux will have had upon the reader; according, as she
wrote to the marquis, to "la manière dont vous en userez avec moi"[6]
["the way in which you use me"]. This sentimental tale is meant to
have meaning, practical meaning, to be determined by future dialogic
interactions among author, heroine, and reader. That action ought to
take place if the author and reader allow themselves to be moved
from one rhetorical position to the other, to shuttle back and forth
from identification to detachment within the space defined by the
genre. In other words, insofar as the "natural" body of each participant in the dialogue has been subjected to institutional inscription,
insofar as that body is a common, generic body, then they will have

been moved. Criticism of one "unnatural" institution, the convent, depends upon the unnatural institution of novelistic discourse. To the extent that the author and the reader "know" that this is only a story and nonetheless identify with it, to that degree will they be moved to action.

It is thus not only desirable, but absolutely necessary that an "unnatural" institution leave its civilizing mark upon one's "nature." Some part of that nature, however, will escape that inscription; to some extent one's empirical singularity will remain a story that no body (except one's own) knows. To that extent, one's experience will not enter into the patriarchal family relations that organize and are undone by the novel. That part will be lost to (re)productive relations, and to that extent one's pleasure in identifying with the heroine will have escaped theorization. That part makes every participant in these dialogic relations a kind of misfit, like Suzanne Simonin, for whom participation in dialogic relations (in the novel) requires a "sacrifice de soi-même."

Analysis of the dialogic structure of the tableau led me to extend that model to cover the general structure of dialogic relations in Diderot. I suggested that the dialogism of these relations systematically transforms all Diderot's texts into "philosophical dialogues" by undermining the law of self-identity that defines the interlocutors. In *La Religieuse*, the interference of laughter and tears, detachment and identification reproduces this model at another level: in each case, one is never certain who is speaking (Suzanne? Diderot? a "man" or a "woman"?) or what genre (a novel or a "true historie") is involved. It is a story that no body ever entirely knows, the story of a social misfit. Neither Suzanne, the author, or the reader (or the novel *La Religieuse*) ever quite fits into the novel (or into the genre "novel"). Suzanne labels as "monsters" those beings who somehow not only fit into the convent but thrive in it; yet from the perspective of the institution, she herself is the monster.

What implications does this "misfit" model have for the political and sexual economy of *La Religieuse*, if not for Diderot's dialogue in general? I shall begin with a "philosophical dialogue" of Diderot that explicitly raises the question of monsters. *Le Rêve de D'Alembert* apparently belongs to the genre, "philosophical dialogue." Yet inasmuch as it is dialogic in the Bakhtinian sense *and* philosophical (insofar as it asks a question about its own self-identity), it does not really belong to that genre. The same applies to all the other genres or types in Diderot: to the extent that they and their interlocutors do not fit into a single genre or gender, they are *all* philosophical dialogues. As a result, if they all escape (self-)definition, they must be "monsters," too.

Le Rêve de D'Alembert makes a striking departure from the rather ascetic tradition of this genre. As practiced throughout the seventeenth and eighteenth centuries, the philosophical dialogue sought ideally (that is, in terms of pure ideation and as an ideal) to get around its own dialogical basis. This idealizing tendency arose from the conflict between the mimetic conventions of dialogue and the demand for a philosophical truth that must in no way depend upon the conditions (such as time, place, speaker, etc.) of its utterance. For this reason, the dialogues of this period tend to provide "unrealistic" labels for the philosophical interlocutors, to present the magisterial figure as a disembodied mouthpiece of impersonal truth and to make his interlocutor into an obvious foil. This conflict also partially accounts for the ambivalent attitude of post-Renaissance writers toward this highly prestigious genre.[7] *Le Rêve de D'Alembert* acutely dramatizes the tensions inherent in the philosophical dialogue. In the *Rêve*, the desires of the interlocutors not only come into play, but form an essential part of the demonstration.[8] In this text, the philosopher becomes a creature of feelings and desires, and these very desires provide the stuff of the argument.

The scene is as follows: after a late-night discussion of "philosophical" matters with Diderot, D'Alembert has such a restless night that his friend, Mlle. de Lespinasse, calls Dr. Bordeu to the geometrician's bedside. Bordeu examines the sleeping patient and chats with Lespinasse about the dream that D'Alembert has been dreaming aloud. While still asleep, D'Alembert continues to interrupt this discussion with more of his dream, which the magisterial Bordeu explains to a curious Lespinasse. Just as the previous night's discussion had apparently given rise to D'Alembert's dream, the subject of monsters now arises from the dialogue between Bordeu and Lespinasse. Bordeu defines the monster in terms of metaphors of weaving or "text," such as "point," "thread," or "strand," figures that designate the conceptual space that would later be occupied by embryology and genetics.

Elsewhere in this text, figures (such as the famous harpsichord, the drop of mercury, the spider, and so on) are labeled as figures. In fact, figurative language in general, we are told, is part of a "poetic" or "female" way of apprehending the world. "Les comparaisons," explains Lespinasse, "sont presque toute la raison des femmes et des poètes."[9] ["Comparisons are almost all the reason of women and poets."] "Philosophical" or "male" discourse supposedly differs from the other genre or gender because its apparent transparency testifies to its nonfigurative rigor. Is the monster a trope, too? To explain what he means by a monster, Bordeu must of course use the "textual" metaphors cited above. The interlocutors locate the beginning of an organism in a *point*, which develops successively into a *fil délié* (or "thin thread": a *délié* is also an upward thin stroke in calligraphy), and then into a *faisceau de fils*. Each *brin*, or strand, of the *faisceau* will then develop into a particular organ. What Bordeu terms monsters are the permutations of these strands, generated through addition, deletion, mutilation, duplication, or imperfect separation of the strands. As the doctor says, "Les variétés du faisceau d'une espèce font toutes les variétés monstrueuses de cette espèce." ["The varieties of the bundle of a species make all the monstrous varieties of this species."]

This sentence has been read as an anticipation of modern theories of genetic coding and mutation. Yet it does not speak in terms of a model to be reproduced and of imperfect reproductions of that model. Dr. Bordeu does not construe the monster as the result of an *error* in genetic coding (as departure from the norm), but rather as *any* of the actual permutations of a combinatory set. Diderot states this notion elsewhere, in the *Eléments de physiologie*:

> L'univers ne me semble quelquefois qu'un assemblage d'êtres monstreux.
> Qu'est-ce qu'un monstre? Un être dont la durée est incompatible avec l'ordre subsistant.
> Mais l'ordre général change sans cesse; comment au milieu de cette vicissitude la durée de l'espèce peut-elle rester la même?[10]

> At times the universe looks to me like a collection of monstrous beings.
> What is a monster? A being whose duration is incompatible with the remaining order.
> But the general order continuously changes; how amidst these vicissitudes can the duration of the species remain the same?

In his view, certain permutations (Siamese twins, etc.) may indeed appear abnormal, but only from the standpoint of a "normal," self-important individual who lacks a sense of natural processes, which are in continuous transformation and flux, as a whole. The normal state of nature, so to speak, is not characterized by stable definitions and contours of species and individuals, but by volatile movement *away from* any such rigid patterning; nature is normally ab-normal ("away from the norm"), and all of life is "more or less monstrous."[11] Monstrosity, then, is the "normal" form of organic life, and as such it is absolutely indeterminable.

I have already already analyzed the paradoxical structure of the sacrificial relationships in Diderotian dialogue. It is the same with nature as with Rameau the Nephew, of whom Diderot cryptically wrote: "Rien ne dissemble plus de lui que lui-même."[12] What a non-philosopher thinks of as normal, transparent, and literal turns out to be nothing but a monstrous construct derived from a series of un-recognized tropes or permutations. Of all the genera, genres, or genders, none is ever more or less identical to itself than is "nature itself."

Thus the nature of nature is unnatural or monstrous, and its identity (the law of its genre) resides in the perpetual transformation of its own identity. As such, nature is something other than a "concept" (*Begriff*): it literally cannot be grasped in one's hand; its identity always flows through one's fingers. To believe in the stable identity of individuals or species is to give credence to what D'Alembert in his dream calls the "sophistry of the ephemeral." When Lespinasse asks Bordeu to define this term, he answers:

BORDEU. C'est [le sophisme] d'un être passager qui croit à l'immutabilité des choses.
LESPINASSE. La rose de Fontenelle qui disait que de mémoire de rose on n'avait vu mourir un jardinier.
BORDEAU. Précisément. Cela est léger et profond.
LESPINASSE. Pourquoi vos philosophes ne s'expriment-ils pas avec la grâce de celui-ci? Nous les entendrions.
BORDEAU. Franchement, je ne sais si ce ton frivole convient aux sujets graves.[13]

BORDEU. It is [the sophism] of an ephemeral being who believes in the immutability of things.
LESPINASSE. Fontenelle's rose, who said that in a rose's memory no garden had ever been seen to die.
BORDEU. Precisely. This is light and profound.
LESPINASSE. Why don't your philosophers express themselves with his grace? We would understand them.
BORDEU. Frankly, I don't know if this frivolous tone is suited to serious subjects.

If only philosophers expressed themselves in more openly figurative language, "we" (that is, women) might understand them better. Bordeu's last words go straight to the problem, which is that of the

serious ("male," detached) philosopher and his serious topic: to borrow Bordeu's expression, the problem of *sujets graves*. They cannot
bear not being taken seriously, whereas other, more frivolous subjects (Lespinasse and the tropics of her curiosity) call for it.

Lespinasse wants to tell Dr. Bordeu about a funny idea she has had,
which she calls an *idée folle*: namely, "L'homme n'est peut-être que
le monstre de la femme, ou la femme le monstre de l'homme."[14]
["Man is perhaps only the monster of woman, or woman the monster of man"]. Two interpretations of this hypothesis would seem to
be possible, one quite rational and the other somewhat mad. Neither
will seem entirely satisfactory, since each explains away parts of the
other and neither can "grasp" the whole. Bordeu and D'Alembert,
the latter momentarily awake, combine to furnish the male-philosophical interpretation of this hypothesis, as *the* explanation of a
female-poetic hypothesis. This they accomplish in a long lecture on
the purported anatomical symmetry of the sexes, in which the female reproductive apparatus is presented as a reflection (although
pale) of the corresponding male organs. For example, "La matrice
n'est autre chose qu'un scrotum retourné de dehors en dedans, . . .
le clitoris est un membre viril et petit."[15] ["The womb is nothing but
a scrotum turned inside out, . . . the clitoris is a tiny virile member."]

This interpretation of Lespinasse's hypothesis in terms of sexual
symmetry clearly betrays the asymmetrical subordination of the female to the male, the female as imperfect reflection of the male. In
fact, as Derrida has shown,[16] this "phallogocentric" bias can be detected in all such conceptual oppositions: their apparent symmetry
always masks a mimetic structure of logical subordination. A reading
of the above hypothesis in terms of symmetry (real or apparent) depends upon attribution of prior, stable identity to either gender, upon taking one as reference point and the other as permutation of it.
Yet the text, as we have seen, provides support for the contention
that any would-be reference point (be it individual, genre, or gender)
has always already been moving away from itself, acting out its own
monstrosity.

A second (nonrational, but not irrational) reading may be offered,
this time in terms of what might be called reversible heterogeneity.
Without the sameness, the identity from which symmetry, equivalency,
or commensurability of the genders might be determined, it becomes
impossible to imagine them together within any concept. No fixed
standpoint can adequately grasp the relationships between these sexes,
either of which is already monstrous to itself and to the other, or

vice versa. Neither is derived or reflected, represented or produced by the other; neither is model or disciple, teacher or pupil. Likewise, in *La Religieuse* those who fit into the convent are monsters for Suzanne, and she is monstrous for them. This literally inconceivable possibility slips through the grasp of Bordeu's philosophy, goes beyond the limits of rational interpretation. Whether one calls it feminine or poetic (or sacred, empirical singularity, etc.), this monstrosity, which the genre "philosophy" must excise in order to work (in order to produce concepts and survive) cannot be conceptually grasped any more than a tableau's beholder fits into the represented frame.

The monstrosity of this philosophical dialogue derives not just from its resistance to classification as either poetry or philosophy, but also from basic ambivalence within the text about its own identity, from the text's "natural" tendency to become something other than itself. Like the subordination of woman to man, that of poetry to philosophy here undergoes a decisive transformation: the "form" is not just an adequate expression of the "content," but also an irreducibly troubling and significant force. Here monstrosity is not only a form and a content, but also the form-content that questions the very rational procedures that make form and content thinkable.

One could also describe the paradoxical status of the *Rêve* in terms of metalanguage. Male-philosophical discourse claims to be metalinguistic: it purports to detach itself from other discourse, to master and control it; it takes hold of that discourse and seeks to "reveal" or "penetrate" it. The notion of metalanguage supposes that a discourse can relate to the world like Diderot's model of the *comédien insensible*: always impassively seeking to capitalize upon those meanings that others have not mastered, trying to bridge the gap between intention and meaning. The *comédien insensible* says only what he means to say, no more and no less. Like the Brechtian actor to whom he has been compared,[17] the *comédien insensible* never identifies with his character but always delivers his gestures and lines as if they were quotations. Likewise, the ideal, if not the real practice of philosophical discourse is an utterance transparent to itself, which has divested itself of all traces of the philosopher's feelings and desires, having thereby achieved total objectivity of the philosophical subject and object. Feminine-poetic discourse, on the other hand, would tend to confuse the lines of control and property (logical priority, literalness of meaning), to break down the difference between meta-discourse and discourse-object. In Diderot, the difference between these two genres or types is never established.

The respective positions of the sexes relative to logical control and subordination take on political dimensions in the following exchange between Bordeu and Lespinasse on the subject of nerve structure:

LESPINASSE. Et l'animal est sous le despotisme ou sous l'anarchie.
BORDEU. Sous le despotisme, c'est fort bien dit. L'origine du faisceau commande et tout le reste obéit. L'animal est maître de soi, *mentis compos*.
LESPINASSE. Sous l'anarchie, où tous les filets du réseau sont soulevés contre leur chef et où il n'y a plus d'autorité suprême.
BORDEU. A merveille. Dans les grands accès de passion, dans les délires, dans les périls imminents, si le maître porte toutes les forces de ses sujets vers un point, l'animal le plus faible montre une force incroyable.
LESPINASSE. Dans les vapeurs, sorte d'anarchie qui nous est si particulière.[18]

LESPINASSE. And the animal is under despotism or anarchy.
BORDEU. Under despotism, that's well put. The origin of the bundle commands and the rest obeys. The animal is its own master, *mentis compos*.
LESPINASSE. Under anarchy, when all the strands are in revolt against their chief and there is no more supreme authority.
BORDEU. Precisely. In great bouts of passion, in deliria or imminent danger, if the master concentrates all his subjects' strength in a point, the weakest animal shows incredible strength.
LESPINASSE. In vapors, that sort of anarchy which is peculiar to us.

The latent threat to this body politic is that of losing its head, its supreme chief, that this excessively sensitive body (*sensible*, like the poor actor) might then be overwhelmed by "female" anarchy. Inasmuch as its definition can be inferred from this text, feminine-poetic discourse would lead to a breakdown in communication: a scrambling of meaning, the crisis state of the code itself. The logical conventions and priorities that make communication possible would no longer hold together. When the actor playing Lysimond in *Le Fils naturel* makes his entrance, when the king of Denmark tosses his hat in the air, at the climax of D'Alembert's dream—at the most intense moments in Diderot, one has the impression that communication has momentarily broken down, as if by miracle.

In "Les Larmes et les rois," Georges Bataille summarized the meaning of these tearful moments as follows:

Essentiellement, *une impulsion irraisonnée donnait la valeur souveraine au miracle*, celui-ci fût-il malheureux. Ce qui comptait, ce que, convulsivement, les larmes maintenaient, c'était, devant nous et pour nous, l'instant affreux et pourtant, malgré nous, merveilleux, où l'impossibilité, tout à coup, se changeait en réalité. Cet instant décidant sans doute de notre malheur, il n'en avait pas moins le sens du miracle, le pouvoir de dissoudre en nous ce qui, jusqu'alors, était nécessairement asservi, était noué. D'un autre côté, il n'y a nullement lieu de penser que les larmes du bonheur ont le sens de l'attente comblée. Car l'objet de ces larmes joyeuses est lui-même inattendu, il n'est lui-même, comme la mort, que, soudain, l'impossible. . . . Ce que je nomme attente, qui se résoud en *rien*, est toujours le calcul inévitable de la raison.[19] [Bataille's emphasis]

Even if it was unhappy, the miracle essentially derived its sovereign value from an unreasoned impulse. What counted, what the tears convulsively maintained, before us and for us, was the awful and yet (in spite of us) marvelous instant when the impossible suddenly became real. Although it probably made us unhappy, it was no less of a miracle for us, capable of dissolving everything which had previously subjugated us and tied us down. On the other hand, there is no reason to believe that tears of happiness mean that expectations have been fulfilled. For the object of these joyous tears is itself unexpected, it is only (like death), suddenly, the impossible. . . . What I call expectation, which resolves into *nothing*, is always the inevitable calculation of reason.

Whether unhappily or happily, for an instant the impossible comes true. Unhappily, the Father (Lysimond) has really died, or happily he (the king of Denmark) is still alive (like the supplement to his *own* statue!): both propositions are miraculously and momentarily true. Both situations come to the same thing: to tears, and to nothing. At these moments, the subject no longer is *bound* by the "despotism" of reason, its "chief." I said that pathos relies on elliptical rhetoric: and the actor playing Lysimond comes on like a human ellipsis, a figure that summarizes and elides the pathetic movement of the entire play. His dramatic entrance makes all the previous interruptions and exclamations seem like a continuous line, which only now has been broken by emergent truth. Before he can say anything, his very presence speaks to his beholders and to himself of Lysimond's absence and of their own mortality. In the Father's absence, they no longer can communicate with each other; what's more, they no longer have to. All of their rational calculations suddenly come to naught: the actors are also the audience to their own performance, but they unexpectedly lose the distance from their roles. Unforeseeably they identify with a translation of their singular lived experience into the conventions of a five-act drama, unforeseeably they identify with a *fiction*. Masters and servants, all forget who they are ("la douleur, passant des maîtres aux domestiques, devint générale"); both actors and play break down in tears.

But only temporarily. For this timeless moment will soon be translated into the narrative of a beholder. After the first performance of *Le Fils naturel*, after Diderot hears the story of the Danish king, after D'Alembert's dream, the climax of each event is transcribed. Each of these stories bears repetition very well: "Je relis cet endroit de ma lettre et il m'attendrit encore," wrote Diderot. In the story of the Danish king, it is also miraculous to see that despotism ("L'origine du faisceau commande, et tout le reste obéit") has been reconciled with Enlightenment ("où il n'y a plus d'autorité suprême"), the Father of the People with the *père de famille*.

* * *

After this excursion into monsters and philosophical dialogue, the sexual politics of *La Religieuse* should make more sense. For example, one may well wonder why the well-meaning, but guilty, lesbian mother superior is made to suffer such agony in the novel, whereas the reader is told that the sadistic, but apparently heterosexual superior is never punished. If Diderot's criticism is directed against an "unnatural" institution, and not against the "Nature" of any given individual, why should the only authority figure who suffers in this story be a homosexual?[20] In the opening portrait of this unnamed mother superior, one is struck by the resemblances between her and the "monster" of the *Rêve de D'Alembert*. For one thing, she is forever out of step with herself:

> C'est une petite femme toute ronde, cependant prompte et vive dans ses mouvements: sa tête n'est jamais rassise sur ses épaules; il y a toujours quelque chose qui cloche dans son vêtement; sa figure est plutôt bien que mal; ses yeux, dont l'un, c'est le droit, est plus haut et plus grand que l'autre, sont pleins de feu et distraits. . . . [S]a figure décomposé marque tout le décousu de son esprit et toute l'inégalité de son caractère.[21]

She is short and quite plump, yet quick and lively in her movements, her head is never straight on her shoulders, there is
always something wrong with her clothes, her face is good-
looking rather than plain, and her eyes, one of which, the right
one, is higher and larger than the other, are full of fire and
faraway looking. . . . [H]er ever-changing expression indicates
the disconnectedness of her mind and all the instability of
her character.

Everything about this character is somehow out of joint, never quite
"together." Alternately haughty and familiar, compassionate and
hard, sadistic and sentimental, this third mother superior (like
Rameau's Nephew) has something unstable or unstitched (*décousu*)
about her. The *décousu* of her character makes the convent that she
heads into a highly irregular one:

> On est très mal avec ces femmes-là; on ne sait jammais ce qui
> leur plaira ou d éplaira, ce qu'il faut éviter ou faire; il n'y a rien
> de réglé; ou l'on est servi à profusion, ou l'on meurt de faim;
> l'économie de la maison s'embarrasse, les remontrances sont ou
> mal prises ou négligées.[22]

> You are very ill at ease with women like that and never know
> what to avoid or do; nothing is stable, you are either served
> lavishly or dying of hunger, the running of the institution gets
> into a muddle, any remonstrances are taken the wrong way
> or else ignored.

It would seem that this irregularity ("feminine," in the *Rêve de
D'Alembert*) and not the superior's homosexuality, this lack of order
at the head of an institution is what makes her worthy of punishment within Diderot's text. In terms of the family- and father-centered
economy of Diderot, this woman is no more fit to rule over a house
of religion than Suzanne is to live in one. Both women are natural
misfits, whose bodies cannot inhabit peacefully under the same roof
as a *père de famille*; both must therefore be sacrificed by the institution.

Like a conventionally successful novel, happy family life depends
upon the consistent application of a law or principle of authority or
authorship. This law need not be applied by a woman, although by
nature it is "rhetorically" masculine: Suzanne's first mother superior
is uniformly gentle and caring toward her daughters, and the second
thoroughly cruel; but only the third mother superior alternately displays the sensitivity of the first and the cruelty of the second. This

constitutional incapacity to submit herself and her family to the rule of law is what makes this last superior into a textual liability.

Like the "monster" of D'Alembert's dream, this character is a figure that cannot be understood in dialectical terms. She shuttles from extreme sensitivity to extreme cruelty, but never do thesis and antithesis come together. The moment one feature of her character is nearly established and has almost conferred upon her a kind of identity, the opposite feature suddenly reasserts itself and begins to impose its contradictory law upon her and her daughters, and so on without rest. At each moment in this abortive dialectic, some aspect of her character slips away.

This shuttling back and forth between terms neither mutually exclusive nor mutually inclusive, neither of which ever quite succeeds in grasping the other, this pattern of nervous movement defines the economy of individual characters in Diderot – the relationships among them, and the relationships among author, characters, and reader, as well. In the passage I just glossed, this was the defining pattern of a single character, the third superior; in the scene that follows that passage, the same pattern defines the relationship between the "disjointed" mother superior and Mr. Hébert, "le *grave* archidiacre" [my emphasis]. Just as each part of the superior's character has to disturb the rule of the other, so the superior cannot help interrupting the grave discourse of this typically serious, paternal figure. One is reminded of D'Alembert, always interrupting Bordeu's explanations. Like Diderot's text, Suzanne is torn between the two tendencies:

> Le grave archidiacre voulut reprendre ses derniers mots; la supérieure l'interrompit encore, en me disant bas à l'oreille: "Je vous aime à la folie; et quand ces pédants-là seront sortis, je ferai venir nous soeurs, et vous nous chanterez un petit air, n'est-ce pas?"[23]

> The solemn archdeacon tried to take up the thread again, but she interrupted yet again and whispered into my ear: "I simply dote on you, and when those pedants have gone I will get some of our sisters to come and you will sing us a little tune, won't you?"

A little put out (*déconcerté*) by this behavior, the "solemn archdeacon" "revint à son caractère et à ses manières accoutumées, lui ordonna brusquement de s'asseoir, et lui imposa silence"[24] ["recovered his usual character and way of behaving, and sharply ordered her to sit down and keep quiet"]. Paternal authority is once again affirmed, though not without some slippage ("Il revint," etc.) between the two characters' identities. This nondialectical, shuttling movement continues throughout Diderot's text.

On a more general level, Diderot's writings exhibit a continuing struggle between the anarchic or "feminine" demands of individual experience (Celati's "empirical singularity") and the centralizing authority of rational abstraction, between "nature" and "civilization." This shuttling movement, this "monstrosity" may in fact be the figure of textuality in Diderot at whatever level one considers. This figure of misfits or monsters describes the shuttling movement in Diderot between the unrepresentable regions of individual experience and the *typical* discourse or body. Like nature in Diderot, like the *comédien insensible* of the *Paradoxe*, Diderot's work in general is monstrous in its incompatibility, its incapacity to fit into the law of any single genre or gender. His texts are never quite here or there (in the *Oeuvres romanesques, Oeuvres esthétiques*), they never completely make sense when considered from any single position.

However much a reader may wish to comprehend what is going on in Diderot under a single head (e.g., materialist monism),[25] he (again, I use the masculine pronoun advisedly) is always losing track of something and having to exclaim, like D'Alembert after the climax of his dream, "Si seulement tout cela pouvait se conserver!" ["If only all of that could be saved!"] Of course, the geometrician was not referring to his conceptual leftovers but to the tangible evidence of his own generative powers. Then again, not all was lost for him either: his faithful companion, Mademoiselle de Lespinasse, was carefully writing down the stream of fertile ideas that were issuing from his mouth. Yet for a moment, it has seemed as if philosophy, the discourse of phallic mastery par excellence, had lost its head; as if the dream of reason had produced a monster, prefiguring political events at the end of the century.

The identity of the text and of the relationships and relatives that define it, this is what Diderot's philosophical dialogue makes problematic in such a complex way. Shall we say that *La Religieuse* is just the narrative, or the "Préface-Annexe,"[26] or both? Does the preface succeed in distancing the reader from the body of the novel? Who is the real father or author of the text? Who identifies with whom? Where does the body of the author or reader stop and the body of the symbolic daughter begin? Only psychotics are not supposed to know the answers to these questions, yet *La Religieuse* derives its most telling effects from implicitly asking them. All things considered, the social effects of *Don Quixote* or of *La Religieuse* place some doubt on the "maturity" or sanity of those of us who, like

Diderot, are capable of losing ourselves in the delight of reading and writing novels.

What is it then about *La Religieuse* that makes a body cry? Like Suzanne's expulsion from social and religious bodies, like D'Alembert's dream and *pollution nocturne*, surely the secretion of a tear from the reader's body is overdetermined. Surely, as in most sentimental discourse, crying here betrays the bourgeois reader's political impotence, his incapacity to do any more than undergo the institutional violence to which he and the heroine are subjected. Surely, therefore, the shedding of a tear also betokens the moral superiority that the bourgois reader attributes to himself by virtue of his rich inner life and his capacity to feel for those less fortunate than he.[27]

Yet despite its patently middle-class character, the realm of novelistic fiction also presupposes a certain kind of detachment, at least theoretically. What happens in fact is that, from time to time, thanks to a detail either poignant or trivial, the reader suddenly loses his detachement from this fiction, finds himself moved by the sacrifices of Suzanne to shed a tear, to sacrifice. At those moments, the reader is being written, caught up in a text that he did not father. At those moments, the power of the author or reader over "his" fictional creatures is miraculously transformed into powerlessness. Where there once had been critical-theoretical detachment, the preface is detached from the novel, the head from the body. In that miraculous moment, the beholder is beheaded, and one cries.

Chapter Five
A Novel World (Bougainville as Supplement)

Let us suppose that a Montesquieu, Buffon, Diderot, Duclos, d'Alembert, Condillac, or men of that stamp traveling in order to inform their compatriots, observing and describing, as they know how, Turkey, . . . China, Tartary, and especially Japan; then in the other hemisphere, Mexico, Peru, Chile, the straits of Magellan, not forgetting the Patagonias true or false, . . . Florida, and all the savage countries: the most important voyage of all and the one that must be undertaken with the greatest care. . . . [W]e ourselves would see *a new world* [*un monde nouveau*] come from their pens, and we would thus learn to know our own. (Rousseau, *Discours sur l'origine de l'inégalité*;[1] my emphasis)

A new world [Un monde nouveau] opens up before you, you cry, and they are delicious tears, you find in your heart unknown consolations, an incorruptible judge and infallible hopes. (Romance de Mesnon, *De la lecture des romans, fragment d'un manuscrit sur la sensibilité*;[2] my emphasis)

The philosophes' fascination with travel literature is well known, nearly as well as their fascination with reading and writing novels. For Diderot and his contemporaries, both travel literature and novels served as means for discovering "un monde nouveau." Each of these genres seemingly expresses a desire to appropriate all foreign experience, both inside and outside of European society. Whether supposedly fictional or factual accounts, these narratives express a desire for symbolic appropriation of foreign experience. Moreover, in the first-person "true histories" written during this period, there is pathos of discovery, typically marked by the narrator's tears. In Rousseau's *Second Discourse*, as in the short essay by Romance de Mesnon quoted above, this desire for knowledge of foreign experience cannot be separated from a certain subjective pathos. In these genres, the voyager and the novelist appear as people who are *moved* to make sacrifices. What moves the reader in the new genre of novelistic fiction is the experience of other empirical subjects; whereas in the travel literature that Diderot, Rousseau, and their contemporaries passionately devoured,[3] exotic customs and peoples nourished this desire. In these genres, movement and being moved are linked.

Perhaps one could show that the pathos of discovery common to these two newly popular genres is only one common feature of a family of Enlightenment discourse. Indeed, that a whole range of semiotic practices, both verbal (the novel, the travel narrative, autobiography, fiction and nonfiction, scientific classification) and nonverbal ("genre" painting, experimental science?) that flourished during the Enlightenment are part of that family. Recalling that sense of discovering (that is, of appropriating) a new world to which our two epigraphs testify, let us tentatively call that family of discourses "the Novel" (with a capital N). In this chapter, I would like to contrast certain aspects of Bougainville's *Voyage autour du monde* (1771), to which Diderot wrote the famous *Supplément*, with the poetics of pathos in Diderot in order to demonstrate the basis for this model, as well as the theoretical problems that it raises.

What were the features of that *nouveau monde* that *le roman* and travel literature revealed to their readers? Why did Romance de Mesnons's reader break out in "delicious tears" as the world of the Novel opened up before him? For what unspoken losses were these tokens of otherness to bring "consolation"? In the previous chapters, I have suggested how the conditions of this pathos in *le roman* may be inferred from the dialogic relationships in Diderot's tableaux, in general, and in *La Religieuse*, in particular. I suggested that Diderot's texts act out a struggle between empirical singularities and centralizing abstraction and that they do so in the context of familial dialogic relations. In Celati's essay *Finzioni occidentali*, this process of familiarization is placed in the more general context of Foucault's work on madness:

> The discovery of the novel . . . is the discovery of a dream
> of global order which certain accompanies the great

seventeenth- and eighteenth-century internment of madness:
the dream of circumscribing all extraneity, the extrafamilial dimension of violence and free intensities; to put it in documents
and report it, so to speak, en famille, to familiarize it with
its internment, placing it within the archives of society,
somewhat as social irregularities will thenceforth always end up
in the archives of the police.[4]

Celati's remarks suggest that at the heart of this pathos of discovery
there was a kind of will *to familiarize the Novel*: to appropriate everything on this or that side of the nuclear family (in the "public" realm,
in the realm of the individual body) into discourse subordinate to
bureaucratic power.

To achieve this end, readers and writers of the Novel (*le roman*,
voyage literature) had to invest a certain amount of adventure capital, so to speak. They had to invest their desire in *unfamiliar* (or
"unfamilialized") experience for the account of that experience to
yield a return, in the form of both knowledge (appropriation of the
Novel) and pleasure (the release of "delicious tears"). Unfamiliar,
"Novel" experience might then be administered at a distance. Readers
and writers of these accounts might then participate in the exercise
of this bureaucratic power—that is, power exercised (by them and
over them) at a distance, by means of documents.[5] Having observed
the workings of this pathos of discovery in the dialogue of a Diderot
novel, I would now like briefly to turn to another major Novel genre
in which the "dream of global order" disclosed itself: travel literature
—in particular, the *Voyage autour du monde* of Louis-Antoine de
Bougainville.

Just as so many early novels sought to define their fictional status
and their reader in prefaces, so Bougainville's *Voyage* defines itself
and its reader in a *Discours préliminaire*. This discourse is "preliminary" in the first place because it stands on the threshold of the
voyage itself; but it is also preliminary because it is almost entirely concerned with previous voyages, with summarizing the results and itin-
eraries of earlier voyages around the world and, specifically, to the
South Pacific. It tells of what these voyagers found, as well as what
they left undone, thereby supplying the pretext for the voyage it
introduces. But the *Discours préliminaire* serves as a pretext in more
than one sense. Bougainville's voyage appears within a context of
conditions (economic, geographical, philosophical, etc.). This context
is the pretext that has made the voyage possible, by virtue of which
it could take place. These earlier travelers have themselves written
accounts of their journeys: in fact, Bougainville continually uses them

as guidebooks; he relies upon them for information, some of which is literally vital (indications of latitude and longitude; weather conditions; sources of food, fuel, and fresh water; friendly and unfriendly natives and so on). Each voyage, in turn, supposes discourse preliminary to it: Bougainville and Cook had read Anson, Roggewin, and others, who had read Drake, who had read Magellan; even Christopher Columbus left for the "Indies" with a copy of Marco Polo's *Journey*. It is as if to every journey there were both another journey and another preliminary discourse; and, inversely, as if every journey were a pretext for others. With the exception of the last three paragraphs, the entire *Discours préliminaire*[6] consists of an enumeration of these previous voyages and discoveries.

Bougainville belittles those of his predecessors who seem to him only to have been moved by greed. For him the history of voyages around the world is the story of man's progression toward certain knowledge of the entire globe:

On voit que de ce treize voyages autour du monde, aucun n'appartient à la nation française, et que six seulement ont été faits avec l'esprit de découverte: savoir ceux de Magellan, de Drack [*sic*], de Lemaire, de Roggewin, de Byron et de Wallis; les autres navigateurs, qui n'avaient pour objet que de s'enrichir par les courses sur les Espagnols, ont suivi des routes connues sans étendre la connaissance du globe.[7]

We see that of these thirteen voyages around the world, none belongs to the French nation, and only six have been made with a spirit of discovery: namely, those of Magellan, Drake, Lemaire, Roggewin, Byron, and Wallis; the other navigators, whose only goal was to enrich themselves by pirating the Spanish, followed known routes without extending our knowledge of the globe.

Thus his voyage joins these previous voyages and discourses in what appears as one single voyage, one single story: the tale (as yet unfinished but sure to be completed) of European man's appropriation of "his" world. For Bougainville, to discover is to uncover, to become aware of distant lands whose presumed objective reality is waiting to be revealed or conferred upon them by the vision of a European voyager. To discover is to appropriate, to assimilate, and thus finally to *cover* the world and possess it entirely.

Both the voyage and the *roman*, then, are parts of that "dream of global order" whose topic I have proposed to summarize under the heading of "the Novel." In particular, we shall see that Bougainville's

Voyage uses relationships and topics that resemble those of Diderot's written tableau but that also differ from it in significant ways. It will become clear, for example, that Bougainville's *Voyage* entertains few doubts about its identity or that of its interlocutors, unlike Diderot's tableau matrix.[8] The long list of previous voyages and discoveries that composes most of the *Discours préliminaire* places the body of the text squarely within a genre, a genre that apparently exists just as objectively as the referent that it is meant to appropriate. In fact, the objectivity of the account is supposed to have been ensured by its mainly practical objectives. The *Voyage* is meant to provide useful knowledge for sailors, not amusing anecdotes for *les gens du monde*:

> Avant que de le commencer, qu'il me soit permis de prévenir
> qu'on ne doit pas en regarder la relation comme un ouvrage
> d'amusement; c'est surtout pour les marins qu'elle est faite.
> D'ailleurs cette longue navigation autour du globe n'offre
> pas la ressource des voyages de mer faits en temps de guerre,
> lesquels fournissent des scènes intéressantes pour les gens
> du monde.[9]

> Before beginning it, may I be allowed to give notice that this
> account should not be regarded as a work of amusement;
> it was made especially for sailors. Besides, this long trip around
> the globe does not have the resources of sea voyages which
> take place in wartime, which provide interesting scenes
> for society people.

Bougainville avers that his travels in the wilds have estranged him from those comfortable seekers after pleasure, and from the "santuaire des sciences et des lettres" (read: the *milieu philosophique*) as well:

> Encore si l'habitude d'écrire avait pu m'apprendre à sauver
> par la forme une partie de la sécheresse du fond! Mais, quoique
> initié aux sciences dès ma plus tendre jeunesse, où les leçons
> que daigna me donner M. d'Alembert me mirent dans le cas de
> présenter à l'indulgence du public un ouvrage sur la géometrie,
> je suis maintenant bien loin du sanctuaire des sciences et des
> lettres; mes idées et mon style n'ont que trop pris l'empreinte
> de la vie errante et sauvage que je mène depuis douze ans.
> C'est ni dans les forêts du Canada, ni sur le sein des mers, que
> l'on se forme à l'art d'écrire, et j'ai perdu un frère dont la plume
> aimée du public eût aidé à la mienne.[10]

> If only the habit of writing could have taught me to compensate

through form for the dryness of the content! But although I
was initiated into the sciences in my earliest youth, when
the lessons which Mr. D'Alembert deigned to give me enabled
me to present a work on geometry to the indulgence of the
public, I am now far removed from the sanctuary of sciences and
letters; my ideas and my style have been irrevocably marked
by the wandering and wild life which has been mine for
twelve years. Neither in the forests of Canada, nor in the midst
of the seas can one acquire the art of writing, and I have lost
a brother whose pen, beloved of the public, would have
aided my own.

As the elegant turn of these final sentences suggests, however,
Bougainville's aesthetic disclaimers are really denegations, paradoxical tropes that (like a fetish) deny on one level what they admit on
another. Bougainville would not apologize for his barbarous style
were he not implicitly addressing himself to someone who (unlike *les
gens du monde*) values both pleasure and knowledge, *forme* and
fond; were he not writing (primarily, if not exclusively) for an audience of philosophes like his teacher D'Alembert—or like Diderot.
This thematized concern for both elegance of form and appropriation
of Novel content would suffice to justify characterizing Bougainville's
implicit interlocutor as a philosophe, but his concluding appeal to
family pathos ("et j'ai perdu un frère . . .") surely clinches the case.
In sum, when Bougainville claims that his wanderings in savage lands
have left an indelible mark on him, at that very moment he distances
himself from the "savage" perspective and identifies himself with
that of the Parisian philosophes who have really marked his style. Of
course, the Bougainville who sees himself as a "voyageur et marin"
expresses nothing but disdain for those who presume to pass judgment on texts from the comfort of their armchairs:

> Je suis voyageur et marin, c'est-à-dire un menteur et un
> imbécile aux yeux de cette class d'écrivains paresseux et superbes
> qui, dans l'ombre de leur cabinet, philosophent à perte de
> vue sur le monde et ses habitants, et soumettent impérieusement
> la nature à leurs imaginations.[11]

> I am a voyager and a sailor, that is a liar and an imbecile in the
> eyes of that class of idle and proud writers who, in the shadow
> of their study, philosophize interminably about the world
> and its inhabitants, and imperiously submit nature to the prod-
> ucts of their imagination.

The man of action sees himself as very different from dogmatic philosophers; he relates just the raw facts of experience, unaffected by philosophical prejudice. Nonetheless the expression of both his new self ("voyager and sailor") and his old one (student of D'Alembert) implicitly subjects Bougainville to the judgment of a philosophe. The form of both self-images reflects the unrecognized image of a philosophical interlocutor. One can only guess whether the results met with the approval of Jean-Jacques Rousseau, who had called for voyages to be undertaken by philosophes ("a Diderot, . . . d'Alembert")[12] if the really important questions about man were to be answered. In any case, with his *Supplément* to Bougainville's *Voyage*, Diderot was responding to a dialogic gesture that preceded him.

The series of paradoxical denials ("I am only a sailor," "These are nothing but the facts", etc.) has the effect of giving the author and his implied interlocutor each the impression of seeing himself clearly in a stereotyped image: the rough voyager, the philosophe. By granting each other a certain authority (Bougainville over the *fond*, the philosophe over the *forme*), author and reader collaborate in constructing themselves and the *Voyage* as objective facts, as data. Neither has the impression of "imperiously [submitting] nature to [his] imagination," each has the impression of discovering (rather than constructing) nature and himself. The voyager and the philosophe both seem to happen upon "un monde nouveau."

This collective will to appropriate the Novel is perhaps nowhere more clearly in evidence than in the naturalness or transparency of dialogic conventions such as those of the *Discours préliminaire*. The conventions that Bougainville and his philosophical interlocutor do not see, that other conventions keep them from seeing, have the greatest power over the reality of which they are a part. We modern readers "see" these conventions, however, and immediately label them as the "ideological" features of Bougainville's text: even though, by definition, we must be blind to our own frames. While postponing for a moment any questions about the unseen conventions that allow us to make this judgment, let us consider how a certain play of "blindness and insight" determines the power relations in this narrative. According to specific conventions of vision, the *Voyage*'s author and reader jointly appropriate specific tokens of unfamiliarity or Novelty.

I have chosen a passage resembling a tableau in Bougainville, not only to heighten the contrast between these conventions and those in Diderot, but also to suggest that the tableau—that figure of dramatic revelation—may be the typical figure of that family of pathetic and appropriative discourse that I have proposed to call Novel. At the opposite imaginary pole to the Earthly Paradise of Tahiti, this passage takes place in Tierra del Fuego. Bougainville sees Tierra del Fuego as an infernal place outside of time ("des neiges *éternelles,*" "une humidité *éternelle*"; my emphasis),[13] older than the world itself: "Les montagnes y sont couvertes d'une neige bleue plus ancienne que le monde."[14] ["The mountains there are covered with a blue snow older than the world."] The natives, whose name Bougainville construes as "Pécherais," seem to live in "l'état de nature"[15] ["the state of nature"]. Now Bougainville knows that they live at the end of the world, though he cannot say which end ("ce point qui finit ou qui commence un vaste continent")[16] ["this point which ends or which begins a vast continent"]. The pathetic tableau that Bougainville paints of Tierra del Fuego reads like a poor (that is, impoverished) version of the episode in Tahiti that Diderot rewrote in part 2 of his *Supplément*, "Les Adieux du Vieillard."

In the margin of the text, Bougainville names this episode "Accident funeste qui arrive à l'un d'entre eux." First, he sets the scene:

> Un de leurs enfants, âgé d'environ douze ans, le seul de toute la bande dont la figure fût intéressante à nos yeux, fut saisi tout d'un coup d'un crachement de sang accompagné de violentes convulsions. Le malheureux avait été à bord de l'*Etoile* où on lui avait donné des morceaux de verre et de glace, ne prévoyant pas le funeste effet qui devait suivre ce présent. Ces sauvages ont l'habitude de s'enfoncer dans la gorge et dans les narines de petits morceaux de talc. Peut-être la superstition attache-t-elle chez eux quelque vertu à cette espèce de talisman, peut-être le regardent-ils comme un préservaitif à quelque incommodité à laquelle ils sont sujets. L'enfant avait vraisemblablement fait le même usage du verre. Il avait les lèvres, les gencives et le palais coupés en plusieurs endroits, et rendait le sang presque continuellement. Cet accident répandit la consternation et la méfiance. Ils nous soupçonnèrent sans doute de quelque maléfice; car la première action du jongleur qui s'empara assitôt de l'enfant fut de le dépouiller précipitamment d'une casaque de toile qu'on lui avait donnée. Il volut la rendre aux Français: et sur le refus qu'on fit de la reprendre, il la jeta à leurs pieds.[17]

One of their children, about twelve years old, the only one

of the entire band whose face was interesting in our eyes, suddenly began to spit blood and to go into violent convulsions.
The poor lad had been on board the *Etoile*, where we had
given him some pieces of glass, without foreseeing the disastrous
consequences of this present. These savages have the habit
of stuffing little pieces of talc into their throat and nostrils.
Perhaps superstition among them attaches some virtue to this
sort of talisman, perhaps they regard it as a protection against
some inconvenience to which they are subject. The child
had likely used the glass in the same way. His lips, gums, and
palate were cut in several places, and he bled almost
continuously. This accident spread consternation and distrust.
They doubtless suspected us of some evil spell; for the first
act of the medicine man who immediately grabbed hold of the
child was to strip him of the cloth tabard he had been given.
He tried to return it to the Frenchmen: and upon their refusal
to take it back, he threw it at their feet.

Unlike Diderot's *Supplément*, Bougainville's writing is still buoyed
by the good conscience of an assertive moment in the history of
French colonialism. The author has no qualms about granting authority to "science and letters": First, he implicitly defines himself as a
figure of science, in contrast to the pitiful ignorance of the Pécherais.
He notes their superstitious nature: they stuff pieces of talc into
their throat and nostrils ("Perhaps superstition . . ."); they believe
in the magical power of clothing, in exorcism and spells.[18] Like
the child at the center of this scene, the Pécherais are ignorant of
Bougainville's knowledge, innocent of that knowledge ("The child
had likely . . ."). Second, in terms of Letters, Bougainville offers
the reader a conventional complicity; he invites the reader to appreciate their joint cultural capital and to join with him in the assent of a
good conscience: the satisfaction of having shared in a classical education (marked by grammar, syntax, and, elsewhere in this episode,
by Latin quotations and commonplaces) added to that of contribut-
ing to the progress of human knowledge. All of this makes for the
moral superiority upon which rest demands for the political and economic dominance of the bourgeoisie: the power of narrator and reader (of "civilization") over the narrated object (the "savage") finds its
ultimate justification in a shared claim to knowledge (in particular,
knowledge of what is best for others) and in a subjective sense of their
own moral superiority. In this fashion, various sets of conventions
(scientific, literary, moral) define the dialogic relationship among author, reader, and represented characters. In fact, the more conventions

author and reader share, the more natural (and less conventional) their relationships should appear to them. One feature of these relationships that resembles a tableau is that they are family relationships; a second, that the characters in this scene cry and move the beholders:

C'était pitié de les voir martyriser cette infortunée créature qui souffrait sans se plaindre. Son corps était déjà tout meurtri, et les médecins continuaient encore ce barbare remède avec force conjurations. La douleur du père et de la mère, leurs larmes, l'intérêt vif de toute la bande, intérêt manifesté par des signes non équivoques, la patience de l'enfant nous donnèrent le spectacle le plus attendrissant. Les sauvages s'aperçurent sans doute que nous partagions leur peine, du moins leur méfiance sembla-t-elle diminuée. Ils nous laissèrent approcher du malade, et le major examina la bouche ensanglantée que son père et un autre Pécherais suçaient alternativement. On eut beaucoup de peine à leur persuader de faire usage du lait; il fallut en goûter plusieurs fois, et, malgré l'invincible opposition des jongleurs, le père enfin se détermina à en faire boire à son fils, il accepta même le don de la cafetière pleine de tisane émolliente.[19]

It was a pity to see them martyrize this unfortunate creature who suffered without complaining. His body was already covered with bruises, and the doctors still continued this barbarous remedy with many a formula of exorcism. The suffering of the father and the mother, their tears, the lively interest of the whole band, an interest manifested by unequivocal signs, the child's patience, all these things afforded us the most moving of spectacles. The savages doubtless realized that we shared their pain, at least their distrust seemed diminished. They allowed us to approach the patient, and the major examined the child's bloody mouth, which his father and another Pécherais were alternately sucking. We had great difficulty in persuading them to make use of the milk; they had to taste it several times, and, despite the invincible opposition of the medicine men, the father finally resolved to have his son drink some, and he even accepted a gift of the coffeepot full of soothing tea.

In contrast to the miserable natives, Bougainville assumes the image of a concerned man of science, someone with the ability to practice scientific method with a heart, who can feel pity for the suffering of another human. His medical science works analytically by isolating the problem and providing a specific antidote to it. The medical scientist couples his advanced technique ("the masterpieces of human industry")[20] with a faculty for pity that ensures the humanity of his knowledge. According to Rousseau (in the *Second Discourse*), this faculty of pity was, along with the faculty of self-conservation, one of the two faculties that humans possessed in the State of Nature prior to reason, science, and society. In Bougainville, the capacity for pity ostensibly guarantees the good use of his scientific knowledge, as if the best of both nature and civilization had been preserved.

Apparently, creatures in the State of Nature may even communicate with civilized beings, thanks to the universal conventions of gesture:[21] "The suffering of the father and the mother, their tears, the lively interest of the whole band, an interest manifested by unequivocal signs. . . ." This spectacle reminds one of the pathetic tableau to which Lessing alludes in the letter cited in chapter 1,[22] where a combination of "perfections" and "ill fortune" was required for a beggar to move a sensitive beholder to tears. Since the Pécherais have the ill fortune of being in the State of Nature, they lack the knowledge required to treat this suffering child scientifically; fortunately, however, the "unequivocal" expressions of this family's sorrow speak to the common, human nature of their civilized beholders. As in many a Diderot tableau, the beholder witnesses a secular martyrdom ("voir martyriser cette infortunée créature"). As in Diderot, the beholder witnesses the suffering of a family and recognizes in the tableau a universal human bond. At this moment, Bougainville's tableau fixes (immobilizes and repairs) reality. Time stops, and for a moment the illusion of a dialogic bridge is created between eighteenth-century France and "eternal" Tierra del Fuego. For a moment, it appears that the spontaneous expression of human nature has come to the rescue of an impoverished State of Nature; as if the basic goodness of human nature had momentarily expressed itself in transparent, universal conventions ("par des signes non équivoques"). The beholder feels pity for "these Savages," as he calls them. It is as if the natural defects of man's origins had miraculously been redeemed, like original sin, by these enlightened Europeans' expression of pity for the "PECHE-rais."[23]

While Bougainville was visiting Tierra del Fuego in 1768, Wright of Derby did a painting called "Experiment with an Air-Pump," which may serve as a visual counterpart to this written tableau. In the words of Michael Levey, this painting shows "a family watching —with a variety of reactions—an experiment perhaps necessary but cruel."[24] The experiment in question is meant to demonstrate that a dove cannot survive in a vacuum. Wright's painting and Bougainville's text share several elements: First, classical composition (the observers in Wright's painting are arranged like witnesses to a Biblical miracle or martyrdom, some of them with suitably awed intensity in their gaze); second, extreme precision of technical detail (in Bougainville, this technical material is nautical and anthropological; in Wright, one sees the scientist's apparatus); third, each shows a family united in pity for the suffering of a fellow creature; and fourth, each depicts an earnestness in the scientist's vision such that he is mythically cleared of any desire for personal gain: his eyes are set upon the unveiling of natural truth, upon further disclosures from a Novel world. Meanwhile, the dove, like the Holy Ghost, seems to preside over its own sacrifice to science. Levey calls this painting a curious union of "science and sensibility."

A curious combination this well may be, but it certainly is also typical of that pathos of discovery so manifest in novels and voyage literature. In the painting, as in *La Religieuse* and Bougainville's *Voyage*, appropriation of Novel experience requires suffering: it requires the actual "martyrdom" of the represented characters (Suzanne Simonin, the Pécherais boy, the dove), as well as the beholder's identification with that suffering. The appropriation of Novel experience requires a *dialogic* pathos.

In the latter two cases, however, the suffering need not be shared; only in Diderot does this effort at appropriation require the beholder's sacrifice. In the tableaux of Bougainville and Wright of Derby, a rhetorical convention separates the "natural" objects of the representation (the Pécherais, the dove) from the "civilized" ones (Bougainville and his men,[25] the scientist and onlookers) and the entire representation from its author or beholder. Like the "civilized" characters, the author and beholder believe themselves separate from the representation. They do feel pity for "these savages" and detached from the *Voyage*, the latter seemingly just the objects of communication, to be exchanged between one previously existing subject and another. Unlike Diderot's dialogue, where the identity of author, reader, and representation is continually subject to question, these two other forms of the Novel take the question for granted. Bougainville and Wright construct and believe in these stable definitions, thanks to an unquestioned set of moral and rhetorical conventions that the early Barthes called an *écriture*.[26] A particular ethics of form makes their discourse look transparent or natural to them. The Frenchmen feel pity for the poor natives, of course, but they don't even shed a crocodile tear for them. Whatever losses the represented characters may suffer, they are not worth crying over. Once again, it almost goes without saying that the dialogic situation in Diderot was quite different in this regard, too.

Beholding this spectacle two hundred years later, one cannot avoid seeing certain of these conventions. One sees that there isn't any clear difference between the way the Pécherais "seem" to use talc and the use of snuff in Europe, or between the casting of spells and baptism ("L'enfant alors paraissant plus mal, notre aumônier lui administra furtivement le baptême."[27] ["As the child looked even more sick, our chaplain furtively administered baptism to him."] Moved by a basic sense of social justice, one may even be tempted to try *seeing through* these conventions, in order to reconstruct what really happened. For example, what if the liquids with which the French doctor probably meant to soothe the child's sore tissues actually made the child swallow the glass? And so on. Of course, if one did carry out this desire to disclose the truth after two hundred years, one would have written a scene from a novel. One would have repainted, or at least touched up, this tableau. From the perspective of a different time and place, Bougainville's narration would have been reframed.

Already the *Voyage autour du monde* had been doubly framed: by Bougainville's *Discours préliminaire*, and by Diderot's *Supplément*. These two narratives frame the entire *Voyage*, as if it were a vast tableau. The *Discours préliminaire* and the *Supplément*—one "before" the *Voyage* and the other "after" it—both follow it, chronologically speaking. Yet they precede the *Voyage* ontologically: they supply the context, the conditions in which the status and meaning of the *Voyage* "proper" may be displayed. In other words, these frame narrations ensure that a new or Novel world will be appropriated in terms of the old one.

Chapter Six
Conclusions

The narrative tableau in Diderot revealed itself to be a highly paradoxical structure, whose frame excludes the same figures (beholder, author) that it requires in order to reach completion. The same paradoxical tableau structure also marks the overall dialogic relationships in Diderot's novel, *La Religieuse*. In Diderot, it seems that every tableau is a virtual narrative, and vice versa. The detachment of the reader from Diderot's novelistic fiction (or of the preface from the body of the novel) must in fact turn into identification—laughter must become tears—for the text to achieve its rhetorical goal. In other words, the beholder of this story is not only excluded from it but also required to lose himself in it, through identification with the heroine. "His" detachment is to become "her" identification. In his desire to appropriate the Novel, Diderot's beholder must finally give himself up. In Diderot's work, neither narrative nor tableau ever quite excludes or includes, ever entirely frames the other.

Both temporally and spatially, the tableau is a figure of sacrifice. Temporally, it establishes a sacrificial relationship between the past and the future, between the sacrifices that have been made and those that it will be necessary to make for virtue and truth. Hence the characteristic tense of the tableau is the future perfect, the tense that makes a past out of the present (or entombs it). "What will have been" is the present viewed from an imaginary perspective in the future: a perspective that simultaneously recognizes the mobility (or inherent "pastness") of the present and claims to bring it all together from a fixed (transcendent), future perspective. It reconciles the fact of mobility (of life) with a desire for immobility (for death).

This future perfect conveys a paradoxical kind of optimism. The tense is optimistic because it points to a time when all the inadequacies of the present—physical and metaphysical—will have been overcome. The future perfect is paradoxical here because the very act of its utterance places the optimism of that utterance in doubt. For the temporal logic of the future perfect tense carries one beyond any future point (beyond "what will have been"). At a first level, however, the Novel tableau expresses an assertive, bourgeois confidence in the possibility of overcoming all present limitations upon the human condition, through a strangely familialized mixture of science and sensitivity. Indeed, our juxtaposition of tableaux in Diderot, Bougainville, and Wright pointed to a relationship between the domination of nature and the discharge of affect.[1]

Within Diderot's aesthetics of sacrifice, the difference between representation and reality became problematic. Rather than lament the human tendency to mistake fiction for reality, or deplore the "effeminate" position one thereby comes to occupy (these are Rousseauist gestures), Diderot positively delights in doing so. Part of his pleasure (as a reader of Richardson, for example) comes from occupying a rhetorically feminine position, from identifying with the suffering heroine: a gesture that, as I have shown, calls for someone else to occupy the beholder's position, and so on. Unlike Rousseau, Diderot does not feel the need to be alone in order to be himself. On the contrary, he only feels himself when "alienated" in dialogue, represented or real. When he avers that "I always associated myself with [those who suffer]; and without my noticing it, the feeling of commiseration is being practiced and strengthened,"[2] it doesn't occur to him—as it does to a Rousseau—that identifying with the representation of a suffering heroine might make him less likely to help someone who really was suffering.

We have also seen some political and philosophical implications of the relationship between "male" and "female" discourses in the *Rêve de D'Alembert*. In that text, the curious relationship between the paternal philosopher or ruler and "popular" or "feminine" anarchy led us to speak of "mutual reversible heterogeneity." The beholder's position is both in the tableau and out of it, framed and framing, both inside and out of two irreconcilable places. When he identifies with a representation of suffering, he asks for someone else to behold the spectacle and identify with him. Yet like the great actor of the

Paradoxe, the framer also detaches himself from every dialogic gesture and delivers it like a quotation. In this way, he hopes to assert his *insensibilité*, his incapacity to identify with the suffering of others. What he actually demonstrates by adopting this stance, by the *act* of utterance, is of course just the opposite of what he wants to prove: namely, that he has thoroughly *given himself up* to others. By marking his detachment from others—precisely because he must represent it, and cannot just *do* it (unrhetorically, naturally)—he also admits his utter dependence upon them. Such is his paradoxical status, and that of so many other Diderotian "figures" as well.

In *Le Rêve de D'Alembert*, Diderot has a metaphor (or almost one) for the beholder's situation. It is "monstrous." I say "almost" a metaphor because Diderot's notion of monstrosity has destabilizing consequences for all hierarchized oppositions; that is, including the opposition between proper meaning (letter) and metaphor (figure). If "man is perhaps the monster of woman, and woman perhaps the monster of man," so may each term of a hierarchized opposition (man/woman, philosophy/literature) be monstrous to the other. Each of these terms is in a monstrous situation. And yet we have seen that for Diderot, that situation is perfectly normal and natural. Monsters are natural, we recall, not because they are natural mutations but because they are the norm. Theirs is the indeterminable "nature" of nature. So when Diderot espouses natural passions against social conventions, he produces a set of natural *and* monstrous offspring: from the illegitimate Dorval and Suzanne Simonin, to J. F. Rameau and so on. It is tempting to view all of the conventional genres (including the genre "encyclopedia") in which Diderot wrote as variants of the same "Novel" gesture, for which the tableau (or perhaps certain plates of the *Encyclopédie*) provides an emblem. In these various genres, reality appears as a bourgeois drama whose ultimate realization requires the beholder's participation, indeed, his sacrifice.

Speaking of sacrifice, we have noted the powerful influence of Christian representation (its conventions and even its affect) upon these typical Enlightenment genres. Before there were tableaux, sacrifice had long been associated in Christianity with images of dramatic revelation and with family pathos. On the other hand, the tableau's relationship to appropriation of nature (through Art) and to framing betrays the influence of a more rationalist, secular position (symbolized in the Renaissance by the institution of monocular perspective).[3] In the tableau, these religious and secular influences blend. In the process, something qualitatively different emerges. A new family of discourse arises, which I proposed to call "Novel" in order to underline the link between religious and secular perspectives, the relationship between the sacrificial character of the novel as a genre[4] and the secular impulse to appropriate "un monde nouveau."

If only it were possible to call Diderot's natural monsters "figures," that is, properly speaking. Paradoxically, what the monster figures is the impossibility of establishing the difference between figure and ground, framed and frame. "All of nature," we remember, "is more or less monstrous." We recall that, according to Bordeu, whoever should fail to recognize the inherent monstrosity of nature falls victim to the "sophisme de l'éphémère" ["the sophistry of ephemeral being"]: that is, such a person succumbs to his limited frame of reference; he is insufficiently aware of his own limits in time and space. This person does not realize that there are specific semiotic constraints upon "his" thought.

This masculine pronoun ("his," "he") suits a framer well. This character thinks he has grasped precisely what escapes him, he attaches himself all the more surely to the discourse of others as he tries to detach himself from it. His "virile" detachment becomes all the more "effeminate" and hysterical, the more he makes a spectacle of it. Not that he could avoid making a spectacle of it: on the contrary, if he did not, he would not be an actor. Thus the actor is a monster, too: not quite a metaphor.

I would like to think of this essay both as a partial reading of Diderot and as a contribution to what Bakhtin called "historical poetics."[5] Having followed Diderot's trenchant critique of metadiscourse in *Le Rêve de D'Alembert*, I had better not claim to have *framed* Diderot. From Diderot's perspective, historical poetics would have no logical priority over its objects. The notion of natural monstrosity that this essay attributes to Diderot makes this very interpretation problematic. Indeed, the project of a "historical" or "sociological" poetics like that of Bakhtin has inherent limitations. And Bakhtin, although he does not (to my knowledge) ever address this point, would surely have agreed with the philosophe here. If anything is fundamental to Bakhtin, it is what Todorov has aptly called "the dialogic principle." This principle obliges one to suspect any poetics, whether or not it calls itself historical, of "monologism"; that is, of somewhere claiming to transcend its dialogic basis. The dialogic principle implies that neither "history" nor Bakhtin has transcendent status, that everything human is subject to dialogue. Historical poetics and its objects are dialogically related, which means that they continue to criticize and redefine each other.

To that end, it will be strategically useful here to examine what

Bakhtin means by "chronotope" in the important text, which bears the subtitle "Essays in Historical Poetics." The chronotope is, he wrote, "the essential correlation of spatio-temporal relationships, such as it has been assimilated by literature."[6] Noting that the term comes from relativity physics and biology, Bakhtin added: "We intend to introduce it to literary history *almost (but not exactly) like a metaphor.*"[7] [my emphasis] Like Todorov, I find this last expression intriguing, to say the least. Perhaps Bakhtin means that if it is not a metaphor (if it is used "properly"), "chronotope" refers to spatiotemporal (etc.) constraints of the real world. As we shall see, Bakhtin stressed the importance of making a methodological distinction between the chronotopes of the real world and those of the represented world. If "chronotope" had been used metaphorically, it might have referred to *representations* of spatiotemporal (etc.) constraints in the "real" world. Here, however, Bakhtin claimed not to use the expression metaphorically—or at least "not exactly." I shall return to this question in a moment.

It has been suggested that chronotope is practically synonymous with genre.[8] But perhaps the term should not be used so restrictively. If Bakhtin's "Essays in Historical Poetics" proposes to describe the chronotopes of a privileged genre, the novel, his examples are by no means restricted to genre. In practice, chronotopes may be thematic ("the threshold," "the crisis")[9] and even (as we shall see below) ontological. The term "chronotope" can be used to mean a particular set of semiotic (form and content) constraints, at whatever level is being described. To translate Bakhtin's term into current scientific teminology is to recognize that "chronotope" has metaphysical implications. It is also to recognize that the question of whether semiotics is a science remains an open one.[10] Whatever the case may be, Bakhtin's emphasis upon time and space (implicit in the term "chronotope") betrays a clear Kantian bias.[11] This makes one wonder how easily the entire project of a historical poetics might itself be framed by Kantian categories.

In the "Final Observations" on the chronotope, added by Bakhtin in 1973, he stressed the importance of distinguishing between two worlds: the one that a work represents and the one that creates that world. Yet he knows that real people (the author, the reader) make the work and that they do so in the real world. The world that they represent, however, is not set apart from the real world, but rather is a part of that world. Representations of the world (ideology) are also part of the real world for Bakhtin. He is not satisfied with a simple dichotomy between art and life, form and content, superstructure and infrastructure, in which one term of the dichotomy reflects (or expresses, etc.) the other. In Bakhtin's terms, the real world and the represented world interact and overlap, too.

Nevertheless, Bakhtin insisted that it is necessary to distinguish between the two if one hopes to avoid the worst kind of methodological error. We must remember, he remarked, that texts are created by the "real world":

> We may . . . speak of this world as the *creator* of the text: *all its elements — as much the reflection of reality as the listeners*, the performers (if they exist), and finally the listener-hearers who reconstitute, and thereby renew the text, all these *participate equally in the creation of the represented world*.[12] [my emphasis]

So the real world creates the text. Yet text ("reflection of reality") is also part of the real world. In Bakhtin, the methodological distinction between real world and represented world is fundamental, granted; but it is also problematic. Like the real world, representations of the world are produced and productive. Moreover, precisely because of the essential heterogeneity of both terms, their relationship is not dialectical but dialogic.

It is in terms of this problematic opposition that we must read Bakhtin's assertion that the real world invests itself in the represented world: or more precisely, his claim that the chronotopes of the real produce chronotopes of the represented world. The distinction may seem obvious enough, but Bakhtin noted (with some dismay) how often students of literature fail to respect it:

> One cannot confuse the represented world and the representing world (naive realism), as been done previously to now, nor can one confuse the author-creator of the work with the author-individual (naive biographism), any more than one can confuse the listener-hearer of various (and numerous) epochs, who recreates and renews the work, with the contemporary passive-listener-reader. (Dogmatic conception and judgment.)[13]

The distinctions are clear enough in theory, and yet in the act of reading even Bakhtin may sometimes fail to make them. Such confusion may be inadmissible methodologically but (as Diderot shows) poetically quite necessary. The *Quixote* symbolizes this poetic strategy, but it is hard to imagine a great writer since the Renaissance for whom the human capacity to confuse "fiction" and reality has not been a major preoccupation. In the preceding chapters, we have seen some of the ways in which Diderot's poetics play upon this source of confusion: first, in the aesthetics of the tableau, where a real beholder is asked to "associate himself" with a representation; then, more generally, as the problem of identifying with a fiction, in *La Religieuse.*

This distinction is also somewhat problematic in Bakhtin. It is obvious to him that the real world and the represented world are not (quite) the same, and it is also obvious that they are not entirely distinct from each other:

> The work and the world whose image it gives penetrate the real world and enrich it. And the real world penetrates the work and the world it represents, . . . continually renewing the work through the creative perception of its listener-readers.[14]

That the chronotopes of these worlds are distinguishable from each other, and that they *also* intersect with and redefine each other — these conflicting propositions seem obvious to Bakhtin. In fact, he added, even this dialogic interaction has its own historically determined form and content: this interaction has its own (ontological) chronotope:

> This exchange process is, by itself, obviously chronotopical: it takes places in a social world which evolves according to History, but which is never separate from changing, historical space. One might even speak of a special, *creative* chronotope, within which this exchange between the work and life takes place, where the singular life of the work is lived.[15]

If this chronotope frames the historical interaction between life and art, where is *it* located? Either Bakhtin's remark provides more evidence of his weakness for transcendental categories (like time and space, if not history or God) or it presupposes that the distinction between the real world and representations of the real world has already been made problematic (in the manner previously described). The former interpretation reinforces the view of Bakhtin's dialogism as a disguised longing for Russian Orthodoxy. Yet while this interpretation may have its validity, it does not do justice to the other, more subversive aspect of Bakhtin. By positing that the real world and its representations cannot ever be neatly separated, he provides the means of making the very distinction between immanence and transcendence a problematic one. If the real world and its representations overlap, the "chronotope" of their dialogue need not, indeed cannot, be pinned down. Moreover, chronotopes are dialogic. Like everything semiotic, they address and redefine other chronotopes. The distinction between historical reality and its representations (ideology) is both inevitable and fundamentally untenable in Bakhtinian terms, perhaps in much the same way as the distinctions between form and content, time and space. This dualism is ultimately as unstable as the categories with which Bakhtin meant to combat all dualism: chronotope, polyphony, carnival, . . . dialogue.

Not that instability need be a drawback, from a historical perspective. On the contrary, shouldn't a *historical* poetics be especially skeptical of any category that apparently remains stable?[16]

Bakhtin would have to concede the philosophical objections that "chronotope" is not, strictly speaking a concept—and that neither is "dialogue" a concept, for that matter. But he could also retort that even concepts are dialogical and not, therefore, what philosophers apparently take them to be—that is, stable, graspable objects of thought. If all human activity is inherently and "naturally" dialogic, then even concepts are discourses addressed to other discourses, and they derive their identity from them. The "dialogic principle," whether invoked by Bakhtin or Diderot, implies that the identity of any concept to itself (for example, the identity of form as distinct from content) is problematic. In Bakhtinian terms, the self-identity of the concept must be as problematic as the self-identity of the great actor in Diderot, and for exactly the same reason: namely, the dialogic (historical?) nature of human reality.

The validity of this hypothetical description of Diderot and the Novel is less important than the principle that a "historical" poetics —which sees genres as social constructs rather than natural genera— must not only display the "historicity" (however defined)[17] of traditional genres, but also cross generic boundaries consecrated by tradition (real/imaginary, theater/novel, philosophy/literature, science/art, etc.) to construct previously unrecognized discourse types (family resemblances). The model proposed here will be modified or rejected, but it should in principle be possible to "discover" (that is, to invent) historical categories of a logical order higher than genre. "Typical semiotic gestures," one might call them. Yet why should the apparently neutral categories of today's scientific discourse be any less historical or ideological than the classical metaphorics of Linnaeus' *Systema naturae* (1758)—expressed in terms of species, genera, families, etc., with kingdoms at the top of the hierarchy? Whatever they are called, these framing categories may have at least as much historical significance as traditional genres.

Afterword by
Jochen Schulte-Sasse

Art and the Sacrificial Structure of Modernity: A Sociohistorical Supplement to Jay Caplan's *Framed Narratives*

I.

Jay Caplan's point of departure in his close (contextual) reading of Diderot is what he calls Diderot's aesthetic of sacrifice. Precisely what makes this aesthetic "sacrificial"? We would customarily label an aesthetic like the one Caplan describes in his first chapter a *reception aesthetic* because it acknowledges the reader's role as a structurally fundamental part of textual understanding. But this label only offers a terminology to compensate for the long-standing omission of the reader as one of three structurally constitutive links of textual understanding: the author, the text, and the reader. *Reception aesthetics* says more about the ideological history of literary criticism as a discipline, with its ontological hypostatization of textual meaning, and about the belated reaction against such mythifications than about the process of textual understanding it wants to apprehend. But even if we take such terminological shortcomings into consideration and change the label accordingly—for example, into *communication aesthetics* or *dialogical aesthetics*—it would share the ambivalent epistemological status of all abstract taxonomies in the humanities that both enlighten and obscure the subject under investigation.

The built-in insufficiency of the term can at least in part be reckoned with if the term is meant to refer to specific aesthetic projects in the past and not to a systematic "scientific" project of the present. Thus, Caplan chooses to scrutinize Diderot's historically specific aesthetic of sacrifice without superfluously trying to contribute to a more abstract discussion of reception aesthetics. Diderot's project is a specific historical form of reception aesthetics that emerged during the transition from an older stratified society to a newer, functionally differentiated one—in other words, from a feudal to a bourgeois society. Shared and codeveloped by authors like Lessing and Richardson, it is the first aesthetic of modernity that in some respects must seem obsolete and alien to us but that nevertheless has had a lasting impact on the aesthetics of modernity—or, to be more exact, on the institutionalization of a separate, autonomous aesthetic realm in modern societies. The preceding statement needs a detailed explanation since it contradicts the common wisdom that the literary project of Enlightenment, including that of Sentimentality, stressed the social responsibility and moral effectiveness of the arts and that only subsequent movements, such as Romanticism, were able to overcome heteronomous determinations of art. My afterword will attempt such an explanation by embedding Caplan's arguments in a broader sociohistorical context.

I will briefly summarize Caplan's findings. According to Diderot's project, the aesthetic process into which author, text, and reader (should) enter is based on a sacrifice or privation of each of the links in that process. To start with Diderot's *texts*: they typically portray a family deprived of at least one of its members (the number of family members "present" might even be reduced to a solitary one, as in *La Religieuse*). Textually, the loss in the family engenders tableaux that display the absence of what is missing more so than the presence of staged figures (meaning dramatis personae, as well as elements of rhetoric and of visual configurations). The structural import of an absence already suggests that the moral effect to which Diderot as a writer of Enlightenment aspires cannot be based, at least not exclusively, on ideological configurations of the text itself. It indicates that the texts are not striving for a representation of morality based on binary oppositions and literary figures as ideological paradigms— figures with whom the reader is supposed to identify in order to internalize the moral content of the story.

The textual representation of a loss indeed prevents the text from being only that, a distanced representation of something else. The loss expresses (on the part of the author) and it produces (on the part of the reader) a desire to replace what has been lost within the broader framework of reading. Being an image of a general societal loss, the textual representation of a loss expresses and produces a desire to establish a relationship between author, text, and reader that compensates for losses within social praxis. But how is reading supposed to achieve this compensation? The loss or absence on the textual level is, as Caplan says, "always implicitly replaced by a silent beholder. . . . what has been sacrificed in a now-fragmented family —the missing part—reappears *outside* the tableau in the figure of the beholder" (p. 22). In the process of reading, the reader is compelled to replace the missing member because the text structurally reserves a place to be filled in by the beholder. One could say that in the process of writing and reading, the desire of the author to overcome a societal loss (and thus the loss itself) is first displaced to the text and from there to the beholder, only to shift again from the text to the author, and from the beholder to the text and the author. The displacement of the loss from one link in the writing-reading chain to the next leads to an imaginary replacement of the loss within every link by using the other links as substitutes for what is absent.

Diderot's literary project is determined by his political desire to foster social conditions that favor disinterested, harmonious relations with others. It is this desire that turns his aesthetic into one of sacrifice. In his *Eulogy of Richardson* of 1761, Diderot writes: "What is virtue? It is, from whatever aspects we consider it, a form of self-sacrifice."[1] According to Diderot, what we sacrifice in being virtuous is an agonistic identity we assume in the struggles of everyday life and the sensuous-material interest we develop within this struggle, which fosters competitiveness, egocentricity, and greed. Diderot emphasizes that reading literature makes us "disinterested." If one takes into account the predominantly economic meaning of the term "interest" in eighteenth-century semantics,[2] then the common use of the term *disinterested* in aesthetic discussions suggests that the reading process is envisioned here not only as a means to moralize individuals but to change the nature of the emerging capitalistic society as a whole. "In his [Richardson's] works, as in life," Diderot writes, "men are divided into two classes: those who live a life of pleasure and those who suffer. It is with these latter he makes me identify myself; and without my being conscious of it, my capacity for pity is exercised and strengthened."[3] Just as the effect of fictive sentimentality is supposed to casually shift from the level of fictional intercourse to the level of reader- (or spectator-) response, Diderot casually shifts in his argument from one link in the reading process (the text) to another (the reader); fictional sacrifices turn into actual self-sacrifices on the part of the reader: "And self-sacrifice performed in imagination creates a predisposition to sacrifice ourselves in reality."[4]

But the aesthetic of sacrifice turns into an aesthetic of compensation. Before I outline this change, the term *compensation* needs some commentary. I do not intend to employ it in the psychoanalytical and sociocritical tradition established from Freud to Marcuse; much less in the tradition of the mainly pejorative meaning it gained in numerous ideology-critical analyses of popular literature in the seventies. The word, which derives from Latin, was originally part of the Roman language of commerce.[5] In the Middle Ages it still meant simply "business." But early on, the meaning expanded into a religious context: Christ's expiatory death "compensates" for the corruption of God's creation through original sin, as Tertullian said in *De prudicitia*. Odo Marquard, who has published two excellent articles on the history of the concept, points to the lasting influence of both the commercial and the religious tradition of the category in eighteenth-century thinking. Leibniz, for example, asserts optimistically that all wordly evil will be compensated for not only in the hereafter but in this life because of God's wisdom and kindness. Overall, *compensation* is a well-established category in eighteenth-century theodicies. The primarily theological usage of the word, though, never led to a loss of the term's economic connotation. Even sacrifice could be called a means of compensation in the economic sense. As nearly all the thinkers of Sentimentality pointed out in their psychologies of suffering, self-sacrifice and suffering not only inflict pain but provide rewards, since they are enjoyable in themselves.[6] *Compensation* and *sacrifice* thus refer to the same economic and religious contexts. But they are more than just traditional semantic currencies still in circulation; they point to a cognitive figure structuring major parts of eighteenth-century thinking. That figure retained its basic structural features even after undergoing a process of secularization in the course of the century. Within this process, the figure's religious structure is transformed into a historico-philosophical structure; the site of ultimate compensation is now seen in a better future, not in heaven.

But such a historico-philosophical projection is, of course, an activity in the present; it reveals more about the present than about the future. Furthermore, if such an activity is at all fundamental for the ideological reproduction of a given society, it is an *institutionalized discursive* activity. The compensation dreamed of in such an institutionalized discursive practice, however, never remains just an object of that practice; it turns into a feature of the practice itself. This is exactly what happened in the eighteenth century: the moral critique of newly emerging principles of social interaction in the novels of Richardson, the plays and novels of Diderot, or the plays of Lessing never had a chance to be politically effective. For the institutionalization of the aesthetic as a separate, autonomous sphere that compensates for the disenchantment of an increasingly rationalized world necessarily defuses the moral or sociocritical content of each work of art.

The theory of evolution that Niklas Luhmann developed as part of his theory of social systems offers, as far as I can see, the most adequate model for comprehending this process.[7] Luhmann replaces the assumption that the development of modernity is directly connected with the rise of the bourgeoisie as the ruling class with the thesis that modernization is more adequately comprehended as a transition from stratified societies (i.e., societies divided according to hierarchies of social status) to functionally differentiated societies. In stratified societies, people belong to one and only one social subsystem, a person's identity being determined by his or her social status. In a functionally differentiated society, on the other hand, a person commonly belongs to several social subsystems, depending on the number of social functions that person performs. Luhmann identifies the century from 1650 to 1750 as the period in which the social system of Europe started to react more or less consciously to emerging forms of social differentiation, thus reinforcing and accelerating the process; the further development of the emerging system required at least partial insight into societal changes and developmental tendencies by the "psychic systems" of that society. These "psychic systems" had to develop a new semantic that could, at least to some extent, "grasp" the nature of societal differentiation in order to make the planning of necessary organizational changes at all possible. The newly created administrative and economic structures that resulted were in turn the prerequisite for the further unfolding of the process of modernization (cf. the administrative structure of enlightened absolutism and the founding of cameralistics as a new academic discipline).

Luhmann emphasizes in this context that the state of knowledge of a given society is never unilaterally and causally determined by the society's developmental stage, since knowledge is not a reflection of factual structures but an adjustment of mental condensations and reductions of "reality" to those structures. The semantics developed in this process guarantee the continuity of the (cultural, economic, and political) reproduction of a given society. But they do not establish a global, more or less homogeneous, semantic or ideological context. Since they are functionally attached to the existence of specific social subsystems, they are gradually differentiated into more or less independent *linguistic* subsystems as well. Semantic differentiation reinforces a tendency all social subsystems display, namely to establish themselves as relatively autonomous functional systems controlled by self-regulating mechanisms and self-reflexive vindications.

The functional differentiation of a subsystem like the aesthetic one usually does not occur as an unfolding of just one such system but of complementary systems with complementary functions. The autonomous aesthetic subsystem that develops during the eighteenth century is, in this sense, functionally complementary to the development in early modernity of technological rationality, of more complex social structures demanding mental adjustments and flexibilities, and of competitive mentalities based on a calculating rationality. Numerous studies from Max Weber to Norbert Elias, Benjamin Nelson, Niklas Luhmann, and Albert O. Hirschman have analyzed this process. But what count in this context are not primarily the changes themselves but the mental structures of eighteenth-century thinking that strive to adjust to them. All major sociological and aesthetic thinkers of the times share a cognitive figure that juxtaposes alienation, isolation, and the division of labor in modernity with an absent and longed-for state of communal solidarity or moral sensibility. Within their own present, they did not see a chance to realize this utopian state; it could be foreshadowed only in the form of aesthetic experience. They projected the realization of this state (the longed-for fusion of ideal and reality), into a distant past or future. But the fusion, of course, existed in the present in a discursive and imaginary mode because it was the subject of historico-philosophical discourses. These discourses make use of a deceptive rhetoric to present the difference between ideal and reality as a temporal difference between a bad present and a better future. Not only does a discursive activity always remain an activity in and of the present, as I stressed before; but the historico-philosophical writings of the eighteenth century are not easily separable from aesthetic writings, for the former tend to perform aesthetic functions as well. Both genres help constitute a subsystem of human activity that, although purely imaginary, compensates for the one-sidedness of activities in other subsystems. Diachronic figures of thought thus turn out to be synchronic in nature: they reflect the structures of a functionally differentiated society and displace them from a spatial realm into the dimension of time.

A case in point is Adam Ferguson's *Essay on the History of Civil Society* (1767), a book that had a major influence on Schiller's aesthetics of autonomy. Ferguson hymnically celebrates affection as a social principle in premodern societies:

In the breast of a parent, it is most solicitous amidst the dangers

and distresses of the child: In the breast of a man, its flame
redoubles where the wrongs or sufferings of his friend, or his
country require his aid. It is, in short, from this principle
alone that we can account for the obstinate attachment of a
savage to his unsettled and defenceless tribe, when temptations
on the side of ease and of safety might induce him to fly from
famine and danger, to a station more affluent, and more secure.

Such statements are cognitively determined by their counterpart.
Thus, they only have to set the stage for a characterization of modern, commercialized societies:

Let those examples be compared with the spirit which reigns
in a commercial state, where men may be supposed to have
experienced, in its full extent, the interest which individuals
have in the preservation of their country. It is here indeed,
if ever, that man is sometimes found a detached and a solitary
being: he has found an object which sets him in competition
with his fellow-creatures, and he deals with them as he
does with his cattle and his soil, for the sake of the profits they
bring. The mighty engine which we suppose to have formed
society, only tends to set its members at variance, or to
continue their intercourse after the bands of affection are
broken.[8]

The tone of this passage is, as is generally true for the writings of
English and Scottish writers during the eighteenth century, still rather optimistic compared with French and German critiques of the
civilization process.[9] Nevertheless, the binary sociocritical figure I
pointed out structures Ferguson's whole argument. It is the pre-
dominance of this figure in eighteenth-century thinking that sets the
stage for the institutionalization of an autonomous aesthetic experience capable of compensating for the one-sidedness of social intercourse in the dealings of everyday life. And it is this figure that
structures even the most important philosophical documents of an
aesthetics of autonomy. Such is the case in Kant's *Critique of Judgment*, when he says, for example:

For fine art must be free art in a double sense: i.e. not alone
in a sense opposed to wage-labor [*Lohngeschäft*], as not being a
work the magnitude of which may be assessed, compelled or
paid for according to a definite standard [*Maßstab*], but
free also in the sense that, while the mind, no doubt, occupies
itself, still it does so without ulterior regard to any other end,

and yet with a feeling of satisfaction and stimulation (independent of financial or any other reward (*Lohne*)).[10]

It is not just by chance that the delimitation and differentiation of an antimodern aesthetic realm coincides with the emergence of a new desire for intimacy and a valorization of human sensibility and sympathy. (Both of the latter terms carried a heavy load of aesthetic as well as political and social connotations at the time). Sociohistorical interpretations of this new desire for intimacy and emotional intensity (and, consequently, of the impact this has had on the history of the arts in regard both to the contents of individual works and to the institutionalization of art as an autonomous social subsystem) used to search for statistically significant social changes around the middle of the century—such as, for example, the replacement of the extended family with the nuclear family. In the course of these narrative accounts, literary historians interpreted the traditional extended family as the site of intimate security, of solidarity, and of communal behavior. This idyllic site was supposedly destroyed by new forms of social organization such as the separation of the work place from the home. It is surely true that the eighteenth century experienced an increased pace of radical changes within the long-term transition from premodern to modern societies. But the most important changes do not have to do exclusively with factual changes in social structure; they concern struggles for mental adjustment to factual changes that might have been initiated hundreds of years before they forced "psychic systems" into such an adjustment.

Furthermore, such a linear narrative (from the extended to the nuclear family, etc.) misjudges the dialectical dependencies of the new wants on newly developed social (and their correspondent psychic) structures. The fact that intimacy was ideologically valorized in the eighteenth century does not mean that before this the same need had existed and been saturated within then-existent forms of community and solidarity. Rather, a relatively advanced degree of societal differentiation seems to have produced for the first time an *imaginary* perception of and desire for unity or unifying experiences. One even can go so far as to say that a lack (not loss) of unity was actually experienced in early modernity; at least, there are enough documents that might be read that way.[11] But this experience does not say anything about the *preceding* state of affairs; it is dialectically dependent upon the degree of differentation our consciousness has undergone, a psychic process that accompanies the process of societal differentiation. The differentiation of our consciousness into divided realms prevents our consciousness from being just in and for itself. It is this structure of our consciousness (i.e., every realm in it is complementary or supplementary to another one) that determines human existence in modernity and produces desires for (complementary) symbiotic experiences. For during the process of modernization, humans obviously underwent increasingly distressing experiences of subject-object alienation. Alienation in the sense of being able to put oneself at a distance from static objects or social praxis in order to classify, analyze, and intervene was, to be sure, an absolutely necessary by-product of modernization. But the emergence of such a psychic achievement had to upset earlier forms of narcissistic balance in humans: that is, to master the new challenges, the self had to develop a stronger superego with internalized norms of self-discipline and self-constraint that, in turn, needed to be counterbalanced by more emotional, symbiotic modes of experience. This emerging need for psychic compensation (which one could call a structural necessity) seems to have generated what is generally called "secondary narcissism," a reawakening and refunctioning of psychic wants of earlier developmental stages, such as desires for emotional symbioses and phantasies of omnipotence, within a later context of culturally differentiated behavior.[12]

As I mentioned before, the most important level of investigation for a social history of mentalities mediating between material changes and complex symbolic configurations such as art is not that of actual change but of the history of word fields and of discourses structured by such word fields. These both reflect mental adjustments to factual changes and influence human actions within newly developed structural frameworks. For the eighteenth century in particular, any semantic history concentrating on word fields like *amour-propre, interest, Eigennutz, greed, isolation, egoism,* and *competition* not only deals with isolated semantic entities but with principles structuring discourses; it thus necessarily turns into a social history and history of ideologies. H.-J. Fuchs dealt with the word field of *amour-propre/ Selbstliebe,* J. R. Armogathe with *isolation* and *égoïsme,* and N. Luhmann with the complementary word field of *Liebe/love* — all invaluable contributions to such a social history of semantics.[13] Luhmann, for example, was able to show that from roughly 1700 on, the code for intimacy was rearranged in accordance with the newly emerging ideal of close friendship and that the concept of love that had heretofore determined the code was being adjusted to the new friendship ideal. Only when the notion of duty had been successfully excluded by (and that of sexuality equally successfully merged with) the new notion of close friendship could the concept of love again determine the code of intimacy.

If such word fields can inform us of principles structuring discourses, they at the same time point toward principles governing the institutionalization and differentiation of activities within social subsystems. They indicate, in other words, the reorganization of knowledge, social intercourse, and institutional delimitations. With regard to the emergence of a separate, autonomous aesthetic subsystem during the eighteenth century, the semantic history of the term *art* itself and its opposition to terms like *technology* and *rationality* are precipitates of institutional changes. The historical differentiation of an aesthetic subsystem made the emergence of a general notion of art necessary. The concept of art as we know it today did not exist before the eighteenth century; the individual arts were not seen as establishing a unified and highly valued sphere of human activity.[14] Differences among the arts were related to their distinct attachments to different realms of social practice. But not only were those arts we still would call *art* today conceived of as more or less unrelated; many artistic skills that soon were to be excluded from an increasingly self-centered realm of human production belonged to the same cluster of human activities as the subsequently valorized arts. The mechanical arts in particlar were soon to be excluded from the realm of the so-called beautiful arts because their skills turned out to be commercially exploitable in the course of the industrial revolution. For one of the structuring principles of the institutionalization of a separate aesthetic realm was the resistance of those arts delimited as "beautiful" to commercial utilization. As Martin Fontius has pointed out, the development of a generalized notion of art and the emergence of a new discipline — aesthetics — dealing with art in general coincide not just accidentally with the emergence of technology as a science and institutionalized discipline: "the monopolization of the concept of technic on the one hand corresponded to an aestheticization of the concept of art on the other."[15]

With this I think we have reached a point that allows us to relate Diderot's aesthetics of sacrifice to what I called the sacrificial structure of modernity. The desire for wholeness that structurally constitutes Diderot's texts (as all texts of Sentimentality or High Enlightenment) and that leads to a structural inclusion of the beholder as an equally incomplete counterpart and substitute for what is missing within the symbolic configuration of the text does not exist to be satisfied. Such a statement indeed seems paradoxical. First of all, it contradicts the explicit ideological intent of enlightened-sentimental aesthetics. On this level, the work of art is reduced to a mere historico-philosophical vehicle for establishing a united Family of Man. The unity, however, that is actually achieved through the aesthetic process is a momentary unity *in tears*, which supposedly foreshadows a united Family of Man to which the aesthetic project as a culture-political project aspires. But the ideology of tears and of a Family of Man conceals the actual aesthetic and communicative structure rather than illuminating it: the historico-philosophical interpretation of the unity in tears conceals the institutional character of discourses as well as the modal difference between the two forms of unity the project refers to without taking that difference into account. For the actually achieved unity *in aesthetico* has an indispensable structural prerequisite that it does not share with the projected unity of a Family of Man, namely that it lacks a structurally constitutive part within each link of the aesthetic chain *author, text, beholder.*

This lack is the structural equivalent of an infinite cycle of desire and fulfillment engendered by the differentiation of society into complementary subsystems. For in a society structured by a logic of complementation, fulfillment has to be broken up into components that only can be experienced successively. This guarantees an infinite cycle of desire and partial fulfillment that can never be arrested in a timeless moment of fulfilled presence. The projected unity of a Family of Man, though, is a dream precisely of such a fulfilled presence in which the circulation of desire comes to a stop. Thus the two modes of unity are in fact mutually exclusive, and there is no comprehensible reason why an imaginary and sacrificial mode of unity should engender an actual and symbiotic one. Rather, the projected ideal, as a focal point of the infinite circulation of desire, stabilizes the permanence of that circulation. The exclusiveness of the two modes, which has to do with the institutional differentiation of an aesthetic and a political realm, says more about the social function of the aesthetic in modern times than any explicit ideological intent of a work of art ever could.

To reformulate the same state of affairs from a different perspective: the beholder can never "have" the other for which the work of art is a substitute; he or she even cannot "have" the substitute, since that would presuppose a fusion of imagination and reality. Such a fusion, were it possible, would not only have to collapse the aesthetic, it would have to collapse modernity as a whole and reverse historical developments. As it is, the distinct mode of experience of bourgeois subjectivity, overdetermined by an egocentric identity with a strong superego,[16] corresponds to an unalterable sacrificial or compensatory mode of aesthetic experience. In order to function, such an aesthetics of sacrifice is dependent upon a constant displacement of desire from reality into the imaginary, from the beholder to the text and the author, and so on. That process of displacement, constantly shifting into a quasi-harmonious circular movement that unites authors and readers in an institution of art whose internal exchanges can serve as a substitute for actual reconciliations, reflects the paradoxical structure of modernity. In other words, the tension between a (psychological or political) desire for unity and harmony and the impossibility of realizing it, of making it real in modernity, necessarily leads (or so it seems) to an imaginary sublation of that tension in the institution of art.

II.

I would like to supplement the rather abstract account of structural changes I have given so far with some concrete historical details. One of the most pressing concerns of the eighteenth-century intelligentsia is the difference between the general and the particular. Basically, this is not so much a concern with a philosophical problem (even if it is presented as such) but one with the quality of social relationships and the changing mode of human praxis in modernity. Sociohistorically and politically, the eighteenth-century discussion of the opposition between the general and the particular as a cognitive figure is determined by two developments.

The first is the evolution of enlightened absolutism as a coalition of economic interest between the ruling aristocracy and an emerging bourgeoisie. The political project of this social formation was to plan economic progress centrally and bureaucratically. In the cameralistic writings of the day, *happiness* (one of the most important Enlightenment terms) is defined as the result of good planning in the areas of external and internal security, growth of population, development of industrial and agricultural resources, promotion of export and restriction of import, social security, and welfare. The realization of this project required the foundation of new disciplines within the social sciences, disciplines that were to follow the model of the natural sciences in their quest for rules governing social interaction. They were trying to understand the role social norms and values play within society and how to impress upon the public those norms and values that were perceived to be most suitable in initiating and reinforcing the projected evolution.

The second development, only partially connected with the first one, is the emergence of more differentiated, complex forms of social organization. This aspect of the development has to be kept separate from the first one because it encompasses not only the results of planning efforts but of the overall process of modernization going on behind the backs of "planners." The evolution of more complex societal structures amplified the context of action that individuals had to relate to in their decisions; it became increasingly harder for the individual to survey and master that context.

Each development had a different effect on the status of literature in eighteenth-century societies. In Early Enlightenment, the project of social engineering led to a valorization of literature—of telling stories—as the most appropriate and effective means of socialization. In his preface to *The History of Manon Lescaut and the Chevalier des Grieux* of 1731, Prévost wrote:

> When we reflect on the precepts of morality, we cannot help being astonished to find them at the same time esteemed and neglected, so that we wonder at the strangeness of the human heart, which causes it to admire in theory all that is good and perfect, while dissuading it therefrom in practice. . . . If I am not mistaken, the reason for this contradiction between our ideas and our conduct is the following: namely, that the precepts of morality being nothing more than vague and general principles, it is very difficult to make a particular and detailed application of them to our individual habits and actions. . . . In the face of such incertitude, only experience or example can safely direct the inclination of our hearts. Experience, however, is not within the reach of everyone, depending on the different circumstances in which we happen to be placed. There remains, therefore, for many people only the force of example to serve as a guide in the exercise of virtue. . . . Every event described is a degree of enlightenment, a lesson to take the place of experience; every adventure is a model which can serve for our instruction, only needing to be applied to the circumstances in which we are placed.[17]

Prévost's preface is an extremely interesting document in the social history of literature as an institution. It obviously shares some major premises of the Enlightenment project of social engineering: the emphasis it puts on "example," "event," "adventure," and "model" implicitly presupposes a transcendental point of reference for all public communication and the existence and acceptance of an institutionalized authority serving as a legitimate deputy of that point of reference. Such an authority will, in case of conflict, decide which narrative representations are the more "rational," "natural," or "legitimate" ones. But in its emphasis on "experience" and "practice," it goes beyond the rationalistic project of Early Enlightenment. A comparison with a purely rationalistic project may illustrate my point. Around the same time Prévost wrote his preface, J. Ch. Gottsched published his *Critische Dichtkunst* (Critical [treatise on] Poetry, 1730), with which he intended to establish an enlightened literary culture in Germany. Gottsched saw very clearly how valuable and essential all narrative discourses were for the enlightened project of social engineering. But unlike Prévost, he never doubted the absolute supremacy of rational, abstract argumentation. For him, literature was a mere cultural-political vehicle in the most narrow sense, indispensable only for the education of the masses (the *Große Haufen*) who were not capable of unmediated rational conclusions. In addition to being valuable only as a means, literature had to be bound to and governed by the more rational discourse of literary critiques. Gottsched's whole project is an expression of his affirmative stance within the broader cultural-political project of enlightened absolutism; he accepted his role of intellectual agent in this system and accepted the epistemological, social, and cultural premises of social engineering. Prévost's preface, on the other hand, shows traces of a beginning rupture in that project, although this is not as pronounced as in Dubos's *Réflexion critiques sur la poésie et la peinture* of 1719.[18] For Prévost, the social function of narratives as examples obviously cannot be reduced to questions of intellectual capacities. His divergence from Gottsched's position becomes most evident in his perception of the opposition between the abstract and the particular and in his introduction of the concept of experience. The incertitude that "vague and general principles" induce does not seem to be accidental to him, as it would have to Gottsched. Thus, the epistemological *and* sociopolitical stress shifts from the rational and the central to the particular and the regional. This shift is one of the first indications of the critical and oppositional (or reconciling) potential seen in art in modern times. Art becomes the institutionalized site of the "particular" *per definitionem*, an oppositional force vis-à-vis all centralizing forces that remains oppositional as long as there is no chance for reconciliation.

In the course of the further development, there was a noticeable increase in the cultural-political emphasis in experience, intuitive knowledge, concrete physical praxis, or regional diversity. Politically and philosophically, the abstract is usually perceived from now on as a force of domination and alienation, suppressing everything "individual." The conflict between "rationalists" and "traditionalists," "centralists" and "regionalists" extends throughout the whole second half of the eighteenth century. As Geraint Parry wrote about Germany: "For the traditionalist critics a style of politics which attempted to shape society towards a single end was inherently tyrannical. . . . Large-scale standardization imposed from above introduced a rigidity into social affairs which distorted the natural, spontaneous and gradual development of social relationships and thereby impaired liberty."[19] Diderot, an antirationalist both politically and philosophically, was convinced that individuals basically did not need state legislation; in the same vein he objected to any planned intervention by the state in the economy. It is his trust in the "particular" that lets him promote what he calls an "experimental philosophy" in which knowledge is not derived from abstract sentences but emerges out of concrete dealings with things. When Diderot talks about experiments, he does not use this term in the scientific sense of setting up a controlled project to establish a hypothesis. Rather, he employs the term in the sense of personally observing, encountering, or undergoing something, of establishing a process that enables us to gain practical, bodily knowledge: "The habitual practice of making experiments produces even in the most unrefined of workers involved with physical processes an intuition that is akin to inspiration."[20] Inspiration and intuitive knowledge assume a mediating role in the conflict between the general and the particular, between society and the individual. This becomes most obvious in Diderot's concept of taste. Taste, Diderot writes in his *Salon of 1765*, is a

> facility, acquired by repeated experiences, for grasping the true or the good, as well as those circumstances that render either of them beautiful, and for being promptly and keenly affected by them. If the experiences that determine the judgment are still present in the memory, then we have enlightened taste; if the memory of them has disappeared and only the impression they made on us remains, then we have flair, instinct.[21]

Diderot dealt with this conflict in narrative form in *Jacques le fataliste*. Jacques's master is the representative of the abstract: he owns a "title" and prevails on the basis of this purely formal (i.e., abstract) claim to domination, but he turns out to be absolutely helpless, and his life is deprived of meaning whenever it is not "supplemented" by experience and practical knowledge that (of course) can only be found in Jacques, representative of the particular. For Diderot, to grant taste, inspiration, and experience a more important role than abstract derivations guarantees that the "general" is not imposed upon the individual. Such convictions are still determined by the belief that the general and the particular, society and the individual, can be reconciled.

To summarize my argument so far: the Enlightenment project of social engineering ascribes to literature a major social function, that of fostering a collective internalization of socially important norms and values. Gradually, however, the more critical thinkers of so-called High Enlightenment detected a danger in the primacy the earlier version of the project granted to rationality and its social institutions. At least in some cases, intellectuals were very aware of the political motives and implications of criticizing that primacy.[22] This critique led to a valorization of literature not merely as a vehicle of social engineering but as an indispensable medium of reconciliation. Literature from now on was supposed to reconcile the interests of the individual with the interests of the general; it was to resist the pretensions of the general vis-à-vis the individual, while at the same time making the individual sensitive toward legitimate claims of "the general." It is obvious that this project still had to presume the existence of a transcendental point of reference that could lend authority in cases of conflict, even if that point of reference now assumed names traditionally seen in opposition to rationality, like "emotion," "sentiment," "nature," etc.

The Enlightenment project of writing narratives for public consumption thus also intended to again bring together personal experience and socially relevant cognition, which had been pulled apart in the process of social abstraction (*Realabstraktion*). This development favored forms of "graphic" or sensuous cognition (Lessing called them "*anschauende Erkenntnis*"). In other words, it prompted modes of indirect, conceptually "veiled" communication that today still shape modes of symbolic reproduction of social formations. A major characteristic of this development is a distrust of words and a valorization of mime, gestures, and acting. In his *Conversations on "The Natural Son,"* Diderot wrote:

> There is too much talking in our plays; consequently, our actors do not act enough. We have lost an art whose effectiveness was well known to the Ancients. . . . What is it that moves us when we see a man animated by some great passion? Is it his words? Sometimes. But what never fails to stir us is cries, inarticulate words, a broken voice, a group of monosyllables with pauses in between, a murmur, impossible to describe, deep in the throat or between the teeth. . . . The

voice, the tone, the gestures, the stage movements—these
are what belong to the actor. And these are the things that
strike us.[23]

It is in this context that Diderot's predilection for tableaux has to
be interpreted. "A mimed scene is a tableau—an animated decor," as
Dorval says in the *Conversations* immediately before he describes the
tableau Caplan uses as one of his prime examples. Diderot's main
concern is the institutionalization of a mode of socialization that is
not authoritative and repressive in the sense that tirades and harangues
in the classical French theater seemed repressive to eighteenth-century
thinkers. He was interested in forms of casual, graphic communication that appear not to reduce the interlocutor's freedom. And because this seemed to be attainable through a semiotic valorization of
the visual, he was one of the very first playwrights to insert long
stage directions and set descriptions in his plays to subvert the
rhetorical nature of the theatrical tradition. These innovations have
little to do with a new trend toward realism, as one often reads.
Rather, they mirror the ideological role of the "particular" in eighteenth-century thinking as well as the conviction that the "particular"
or sensuous cognition cannot be so easily appropriated as a means of
domination as the rhetorical discourses of classical French theater.

This change in the mode of symbolic reproduction of social formations is connected with the transition from stratified to functionally
differentiated societies. Stratified societies relied in their ideological
reproduction upon external authoritarian control. Linguistically,
they relied upon more direct and thus more repressive and authoritative rules of conduct; the phrase "Thou shalt not . . ." is characteristic for the educational attitude behind the secular literature of
proper behavior and the religious tracts dominating the book market
in the seventeenth and early eighteenth centuries, even if the phrase
is seldom directly used. These literatures were the discursive equivalent of political and religious domination by authoritative institutions.

During the transition from external and repressive to internalized
forms of ideological reproduction, new forms of religious belief developed that allowed the individual to establish direct contact with
God, evading the church as mediator. Secular narratives could develop into a predominant medium of socialization only when the transition from stratified to functionally differentiated societies had reached
a stage that required secular, nonrepressive, and casual internalizations
of norms and values and a higher degree of autonomous behavior.[24]
The establishment of such a medium did not, of course, succeed
without major conflicts and struggles. At the beginning of the century,

numerous ministers, fearing the loss of their educational privileges, wrote polemics against secular narratives. And philosophers like Helvétius and Holbach who believed that "man was absolutely controlled by the principle of self-interest" could not accept the "notion of an independent internal regulating mechanism,"[25] which was a precondition for the valorization of literature as a predominant medium of socialization.

The institutionalization of the aesthetic as safe retreat and protector of the "particular" soon became exposed to its very own dialectic of enlightenment, which one could call a dialectic of sentimentality. The dialectic of reason as described by Horkheimer and Adorno means the indistinguishable unity of rationality as a power of liberation and suppression. "Enlightenment dissolves the injustice of the old inequality—unmediated lordship and mastery—but at the same time perpetuates it in universal mediation, in the relation of any one existent to any other."[26] That mediation was achieved with the tools of abstraction and formal logic. "To the Enlightenment, that which does not reduce to numbers . . . becomes illusion; modern positivism writes it off as literature."[27] But this strategy of exclusion, this thinking in oppositional terms, in which only the rational is conceived of as general, concealed the fact that from the beginning the aesthetic as a differentiated subsystem with a specific social function contributed to another process of generalization and standardization, namely that of the emotional. To fulfill its structural function of being a realm of compensation, the aesthetic had to be appropriated as a vehicle of generalization as well. Again, we have to distinguish between two levels on which generalization took place. Usually when we talk about emotional standardization through aesthetic works, we think of reading particular texts (contents) and of their specific effects on human norms and values. When Horkheimer and Adorno assail the feature of "universal mediation" in modern societies and speak of the "unity of the manipulated collective,"[28] they argue with regard to the standardized contents of individual works. But "generalization" took place on an institutional level as well; it is much harder to resist this mode of generalization, which structures our intercourse with the aesthetic as a relatively independent subsystem.

A differentiated, institutionalized aesthetic realm was unfit as a refuge of the "particular" because of the structure of modernity and not because of a historical development gone wrong. When Caplan writes that Diderot's theater of the imagination and of the spectacle "corresponds to the declining importance of the public sphere, in literature and elsewhere" (p. 37), he momentarily puts insufficient emphasis on the fundamentally precarious status of the aesthetic in modernity. When the reader becomes absorbed in the aesthetic and sacrifices his agonistic identity in order to experience imaginary modes of symbiosis, he indeed "is being written, caught up in a text that he did not father." (p. 75) And the powerlessness thus established is indeed a sacrifice, a surrendering, a giving up. At a closer look, though, we can distinguish two modes of sacrifice taking place at the same time; they are absolutely parallel to the two modes of generalization I talked about: the sacrifice of individuality in the process of "being written," and the sacrifice of agonistic identity in the institutionalized commerce with the aesthetic. The first form of sacrifice takes place on the textual level—on the level of reader responses to individual works. This form of sacrifice, a precondition for the development of abstract identity in modernity, is the one discussed and more or less comprehended by eighteenth-century contemporaries. It is the form that led Diderot to state: "La vertu est un sacrifice de soi-même." The second form of sacrifice, which contemporaries did not comprehend, takes place on the institutional level.

But the nature of sacrifice has been secularized in both cases. Sacrifice used to be viewed and practiced as a transgression of time and space. Under the historical conditions of abstract socialization, sacrifice has changed, on the one hand, into a form of negation or elimination *within* the boundaries of time and space where only individuality is being transgressed and, on the other hand, into temporal displacements in which only the moment is transgressed. In other words, sacrifice as an institutionalized mode of intercourse with the aesthetic (the functionally more essential mode of sacrifice in modernity) always can and will be reversed because it is profoundly temporary.

Notes

Notes

Introduction

1. Diderot, *Le Neveu de Rameau* (Paris: Editions Sociales, 1972), 90.

2. In the introduction to her reading of Diderot's rhetoric, Carol Sherman writes: "In the search for the coherence of his literary production, many have observed its fundamentally dialogic nature." Although there are countless studies of dialogue in particular Diderot texts, Sherman's excellent book (*Diderot and the Art of Dialogue* [Geneva: Droz, 1976], 11) is the only one that undertakes a synthetic view of the problem. On the dialogic relationship in Diderot, see also Herbert Dieckmann, *Cinq leçons sur Diderot* (Geneva: Droz, 1959); Jean Starobinski, "Diderot et la parole des autres," *Critique* 296 (1972): 3-22; Herbert Josephs, *Diderot's Dialogue of Language and Gesture: Le Neveu de Rameau* (Columbus: Ohio State University Press, 1969), Christie Vance McDonald, "Le Dialogue, l'utopie: le *Supplément au Voyage de Bougainville* par Denis Diderot," *Canadian Review of Comparative Literature* 3 (Winter 1976): 63-74; James Creech, "Diderot and the Pleasure of the Other: Friends, Readers, and Paternity," *Eighteenth-Century Studies* 11 (Summer 1977): 439-56; and Lucette Finas, "Les Brelandières de Diderot," *Poésie* 14 (1980): 77-107.

3. Cf. Emile Benveniste, *Problèmes de linguistique générale* (Paris: Gallimard, 1966), 251-66; Jacques Lacan, *Ecrits* (Paris: Seuil, 1966); and Anthony Wilden, *System and Structure: Essays in Communication and Exchange* (London: Tavistock, 1972).

4. On the philosophical status of paradox in Diderot, see Philippe Lacoue-Labarthe, "Diderot, le paradoxe et la mimesis," *Poétique* 43 (1980): 267-81; and Virginia E. Swain, "Diderot's *Paradoxe sur le comédien*: The paradox of reading," *Studies on Voltaire and the Eighteenth Century* 208 (1982): 1-71.

5. Lacoue-Labarthe, "Diderot, le paradoxe," 267.

6. Michael Fried, *Absorption and Theatricality: Painting and Beholder in the Age of Diderot* (Berkeley: University of California Press, 1980).

7. Cf. Sherman (*Diderot*, 150): "The entire conversation draws a conclusion or reaction from an interlocutor who is both outsider and participant—his reader."

8. Cf. Jean Varloot's introduction to Diderot, *Le Rêve de D'Alembert* (Paris: Editions Sociales, 1971), xcviii.

9. Diderot, *Rameau's Nephew and Other Works* (Indianapolis: Bobbs-Merrill, 1975), 9. Translations from *Le Neveu* in the following chapters are taken from this edition.

10. Tzvetan Todorov, *Mikhaïl Bakhtine, le principe dialogique* (Paris: Seuil, 1981), 98. Bakhtin's views have become better known in recent years outside of the Soviet Union, thanks to a rapidly increasing number of translations and critical studies. In particular, Todorov's study provides an important synthesis of Bakhtin's work along with copious amounts of previously untranslated material. A translation (by Wlad Godzich) of this work has recently appeared: *Mikhail Bakhtin: The Dialogical Principle* (Minneapolis, Minn.: University of Minnesota Press, 1984). See also M. M. Bakhtin, *The Dialogic Imagination*, trans. Caryl Emerson and Michael Holquist (Austin: University of Texas Press, 1981); P. N. Medvedev and M. M. Bakhtin, *The Formal Method in Literary Scholarship: A Critical Introduction to Sociological Poetics*, transl. Albert J. Wehrle (Baltimore: Johns Hopkins University Press, 1978); and V. N. Voloshinov, *Marxism and the Philosophy of Language*, transl. L. Matejka and I. R. Titunik (New York: Seminar Press, 1973). Cf. also David Carroll's excellent review article on these recent publications, "The Alterity of Discourse: Form, History, and the Question of the Political in M. M. Bakhtin," *Diacritics* 13 (Summer 1983): 65-83.

11. Todorov, *Mikhail Bakhtin: The Dialogical Principle*, 60-74.

12. On Diderot's materialism, see Marx Wartofsky, "Diderot and the Development of Materialist Monism," *Diderot Studies* 2 (1952): 279-329; Varloot, Introduction to *Le Rêve de D'Alembert*; as well as Elisabeth de Fontenay's important new book, *Diderot, ou le matérialisme enchanté* (Paris: Grasset, 1981).

13. See Dieckmann, *Cinq leçons*; Starobinski, "Diderot et la parole"; and Creech, "Diderot and the Pleasure."

14. See below, especially chapters 1, 2, and 4.

15. "Les *Principes* et les dialogues consacrent la rupture définitive du matérialisme avec le mécanisme." Varloot, Introduction to *Le Rêve de D'Alembert*, xcvii. See also Herbert Dieckmann, *Die künstlerische Form des Rêve de D'Alembert* (Cologne and Upladen: Westdeutscher Verlag, 1966).

16. As Wartofsky put it in 1952: "Diderot's place in the history of philosophy too often suffers the common fate of the allegedly shallow philosophical writings of eighteenth-century France." "Diderot and the Development," 280.

17. Diderot, *Oeuvres esthétiques* [hereinafter referred to as *O. E.*] (Paris: Garnier, 1968), 32.

18. Ibid., 33.
19. Ibid., 30.
20. Ibid., 38.
21. Ibid., 33.

22. Cf. Jean Starobinski, "L'Immortalité mélancolique," *Le Temps de la refléxion* 3 (1982): 231-51.

23. In *Tom Jones*, for example, Miss Sophia Western tells her aunt that the novel she is reading has "cost" her many a tear: "Ay, and do you love to cry then?" says the aunt. "I love a tender sensation," answered the niece, "and would pay the price of a tear for it at any time." Henry Fielding, *The History of Tom Jones* (New York, Modern Library: 1950), 229 [book 6, chap. 5].

24. *O. E.*, 189.
25. Ibid., 31.
26. Ibid., 194.

27. Jacques Chouillet, *La Formation des idées esthétiques de Diderot* (Paris: P.U.F., 1973), 442 ff.

Chapter 1. The Aesthetics of Sacrifice

1. *O.E.*, 99.
2. Ibid., 88.
3. Ibid.
4. Cf. Fried, *Absorption and Theatricality.*
5. *O.E.*, 89.
6. Ibid.
7. Henri Gouhier interprets Pascal's use of the "Memorial" as a means of repeatedly coming to terms with the absence of the Father, in *Blaise Pascal: Commentaires* (Paris: Vrin, 1971). I shall have numerous occasions to point out resemblances between the sacrificial structure of Diderot's tableaux and the Christian iconographic tradition. For a brilliant interpretation of the relationship between Christian tradition and images, cf. Jean-Joseph Goux, *Les Iconoclastes* (Paris: Seuil, 1977).
8. Gilles Deleuze, *Présentation de Sacher-Masoch* (Paris: Minuit, 1967), 28-29. English translation by Jean McNeil, in Deleuze, *Masochism: An interpretation of coldness and cruelty* (New York: G. Braziller, 1971).
9. *O.E.*, 115-16.
10. Ibid., 116.
11. Ibid., 31.
12. Georges Bataille, *L'Erotisme* (Paris: Minuit, 1957).
13. According to Peter Szondi, Diderot's preference for the tableau over the sudden turns of fortune that French Classical theater called *coups de théâtre* was based upon an implicit recognition that the *coup de théâtre*, as a theatrical device, presupposed the logic of feudal relations; that is, the logic of a feudal society where alliances are constantly shifting and the goddess Fortuna plays a decisive role. Moreover, the *coup de théâtre* belongs to a fundamentally public society, whereas the tableau bears witness to the newer privatized, bourgeois form of society, organized around the nuclear family. Laying particular emphasis upon the scene of reconciliation with which *Le Père de famille* concludes, Szondi maintains that its conventionality, now pressed into the service of sentimentality, acquires a new meaning in this context. In Szondi's view, sentimentality and the cult of private virtue betoken the political impotence of the bourgeoisie in France: "As long as the bourgeoisie does not revolt against absolutism and make a bid for power, it will live solely for its emotions, bewailing in the theater its own misery, which is inflicted upon it, as Diderot observed, as much by men as the misery of the heroes of Attic tragedy was inflicted upon them by fate." *"Tableau* and *coup de théâtre,"* *New Literary History* 11 (Winter 1980): 340. For a more extensive discussion of Diderot, reconstructed from lecture notes by Szondi's students, see: "Denis Diderot: Theorie und dramatische Praxis," in *Die Theorie des bürgerlichen Trauerspiels* (Frankfurt: Suhrkampf, 1974), 91-147.
14. *O.E.*, 189.
15. Ibid., 90.
16. Szondi, "Denis Diderot," 105-6.
17. Cf. Erich Auerbach, "The Interrupted Supper," in *Mimesis* (Princeton, N.J.: Anchor, 1957), 350. Here the great philologist takes note of "the then fashionable thrill of mingled sentiment and eroticism" in *Manon Lescaut.*
18. Szondi, "Denis Diderot," 116.
19. *O.E.*, 89.
20. Fried, *Absorption and Theatricality.*

21. In *La Formation des idées esthétiques*, Chouillet interprets this conflict in *Le Père de famille* as an opposition between two images of the family: "d'une part la famille 'légale', lieu de l'ignorance et du préjugé-elle est représentée, si l'on veut par le Commandeur—, et d'autre part, la famille 'naturelle', lieu des sentiments vrais. Entre les deux le personnage du Père, qu'on va s'arranger pour faire passer d'un groupe à l'autre." (470)

22. Quoted in Szondi, *"Tableau* and *coup de théâtre,"* 336.

23. I borrow this expression from Serge Leclair's definition of the "letter" in psychoanalysis: "trait qui constitue et marque, en un lieu du corps, l'affleurement de la jouissance dans l'immédiateté d'une différence exquise." *Psychanalyser* (Paris: Seuil, 1968), 74.

24. Cf. Arnold Hauser's description of the new bourgeois reading public that arose in England toward the end of the seventeenth century, in *The Social History of Art* (New York, Vintage Books, n.d.), vol. 3, 38-84.

25. *O.E.*, 311.

26. *O.E.*, 196.

27. Diderot, *Le Neveu de Rameau*, 96. Cf. also Jeffrey Mehlman, *Cataract: A Study in Diderot* (Middletown, Conn.: Wesleyan University Press, 1979), chap. 4.

28. Diderot, *Le Neveu de Rameau*, 97.

29. Ibid., 97-98.

30. Ibid., 110.

31. Ibid., 98, note 1. Letter to Sophie Volland dated 31 July 1762.

32. Ibid., 99.

33. Ibid.

34. Ibid. On the "tree" metaphor, cf. Chouillet, *La Formation des idées esthétiques*, 387.

35. Diderot, *Le Neveu de Rameau*, 99. In chapter 2, I analyze a similar passage in Diderot's letter to Sophie of 25 July 1762 ("L'histoire de cette journée fera verser des larmes de joie dans deux cents ans, dans mille ans d'ici.")

36. See Chouillet, *La Formation des idées esthétiques*, 454-62, as well as his *Diderot* (Paris: C.E.D.E.S., 1977), 150-52. Szondi ("Denis Diderot," 114) claims that *Le Fils naturel* testifies to the state of tragedy in eighteenth-century France rather than to Diderot's incapacity to understand tragedy.

37. Chouillet, *Diderot*, 151.

38. *O.E.*, 147, note 1. Szondi, "Denis Diderot."

Chapter 2. Genealogy of the Beholder

1. Diderot, *Oeuvres complètes* (*Le Drame bourgeois*), [hereinafter referred to as *O.C.*] 6.

2. Ibid., 7-8.

3. Chouillet, *La Formation des idées esthétiques*, 470 ff.

4. Ibid., 471. Cf. Maurice Descotes, *Le Public de théâtre et son histoire* (Paris: P.U.F., 1964), chap. 6.

5. *O.C.*, vol. 10, 16.

6. Ibid.

7. See below, 37-39.

8. Szondi, "Denis Diderot," 115. Cf. also Mehlman, *Cataract*, 33-34; as well as Jack Undank, *Diderot: Inside, outside, and in-between* (Madison: Coda Press, 198), 95 ff.

9. E. K. Chambers, *The Medieval Stage* (London: Oxford University Press, 1925 ed.), vol. 2, chap. 22. I wish to thank Wlad Godzich for having brought this parallel to my attention.

10. Ibid., 160.

11. Diderot, *O.C.*, vol. 10, 89.

12. Cf. Jürgen Habermas, *Strukturwandel der Offentlichkeit: Untersuchungen zu einer Kategorie der Bürgerlichen Gesellschaft* (Darmstadt and Neuwied: Luchterhand, 1962); as well as Philippe Ariès, *L'Enfant et la vie familiale sous l'ancien régime* (Paris: Plon, 1960).

13. Josephs, *Diderot's Dialogue*, Roger Kempf, *Diderot et le roman* (Paris: Seuil, 1964), 105.

14. Szondi, "Denis Diderot."

15. Assézat-Tourneux edition of Diderot, *Oeuvres completes*, 19, 79.

16. Diderot's conviction in the essential mobility of nature is expressed in numerous places, notably in the *Lettre sur les aveugles*, *De l'interprétation de la nature*, and *Le Rêve de D'Alembert*. See below, chapter 4.

17. But the Protestant Rousseau did not share Diderot's confidence in the redemptive power of images. Cf. Goux, *Les Iconclastes*.

18. Jacques Derrida, *De la grammatologie* (Paris: Seuil, 1967).

Chapter 3. Moving Pictures (La Religieuse—I)

1. Assézat-Tourneux, 5, 175-76.

2. Cf. Georges May, *Diderot et la Religieuse* (New Haven, Conn., and Paris: Yale University Press and P.U.F., 1954), as well as May's introduction to the edition of *La Religieuse* that he has annotated for the Hermann edition of the *Oeuvres complètes*, 11 (Paris, 1975), 3-12. All subsequent references to *La Religieuse* will be to this edition.

3. See Dieckmann's introduction to the preface of *La Religieuse*, in the Hermann edition, 15-21, for a slightly different interpretation of these circumstances.

4. Antoine Adam, "Introduction," *Romanciers du XVIIe siècle* (Paris: Pléaide, 1958), 7.

5. Michel Foucault, *Histoire de la folie à l'âge classique* (Paris: Gallimard, 1972).

6. Gianni Celati, *Finzioni occidentali* (Turin: Einaudi, 1975).

7. Ibid., 42-43.

8. *La Religieuse*, 30.

9. Ibid., 31.

10. Ibid., 81. Cf. Georges May's "Appendice," ibid., 289; Jean Macary, "Structure dialogique de *La Religieuse* de Diderot," in *Essays on the Age of Enlightenment in Honor of Ira O. Wade*, ed. Jean Macary (Geneva: Droz, 1977), 193-204. In the latter article, Macary (citing Todorov) notes the relationship between the ambiguity of *La Religieuse* and its dialogism.

11. Celati, *Finzioni occidentali*. Moll Flanders's testimony is not her own language but the result of an author's normative choices. In fact, the "author," in the modern sense, emerges here as the figure legally responsible for introducing certain assertions into the world.

12. For an interesting psychological approach to this problem, see Herbert Josephs, "Diderot's *La Religieuse*: Libertinism and the Dark Night of the Soul," *MLN* 91 (1976): 734-55.

13. "L'hypotypose est un mot grec qui signifie *image, tableau*. C'est lorsque dans les descriptions on peint les faits dont on parle, come si ce qu'on dit était actuèlement devant les yeux." Dumarsais-Fontanier, *Les Tropes* (Geneva: Slatkine Reprints, 1967), vol. 1, 151.

14. Translation by Leonard Tancock, in Diderot, *The Nun* (Middlesex: Penguin, 1974), 27. All subsequent translations from *La Religieuse* are taken from this edition.

15. Ibid.

16. Ibid., 31.

17. Ibid., 231.

18. Herbert Josephs' 1976 article "Diderot's *La Religieuse*" develops the erotic side of *La Religieuse* in interesting ways.

19. *La Religieuse*, 193.

20. Hans Robert Jauss, *Aesthetic Experience and Literary Hermeneutics* (Minneapolis: University of Minnesota Press, 1982), 153.

21. Todorov, *Mikhail Bakhtin: The Dialogical Principle*, 56.

22. Cf. Hauser, *Social History of Art*, 38-87. In this regard, cf. Norbert Elias' suggestions for further research into the social reorganization of affect in the eighteenth century, in *Die Höfische Gesellschaft* (Neuwied and Berlin: Luchterhand, 1969), 170 ff.

23. Celati, *Finzioni occidentali*, 25-28.

24. *La Religieuse*, 46.

25. Ibid., 270. Cf. also V. Mylne, "What Suzanne knew: Lesbianism and *La Religieuse*," *Studies on Voltaire and the Eighteenth Century* 208 (1982): 167-73.

26. *La Religieuse*, 236-37.

27. Georges Bataille, *Le Bleu du ciel* (Paris: Pauvert, 1957), 7-8.

Chapter 4. Misfits (La Religieuse—II)

1. *La Religieuse*, 184.

2. Ibid., 183.

3. Ibid., 183-84.

4. Ibid.

5. In part 3 of the *Supplément*, the Tahitian Ourou calls marital fidelity unnatural, contrary to "the general law of things": Diderot, *Oeuvres philosophiques* (Paris: Garnier, 1964), 480.

6. *La Religieuse*, 92.

7. Maurice Roelens, "Le Dialogue philosophique, genre impossible," *Cahiers de l'Association internationale d'Etudes Françaises* 24 (1972): 43-58.

8. Of course, this tendency culminates in the writings of Sade. Cf. Henri Blanc's Bakhtinian approach to Sade, "Sur le statut du dialogue dans l'oeuvre de Sade," *XVIIIème Siècle* 4 (1972): 301-14.

9. *Le Rêve de D'Alembert*, 57. Jean Varloot has written a very helpful introduction to his edition of the Leningrad manuscript; cf. the Introduction to the present work, note 8. One should also consult Dieckmann's *Die künstlerische Form* and the articles by Dieckmann, Georges May, Aram Vartanian, and others in *Diderot Studies* 17 (1973).

10. Assézat-Tourneux, 9, 418.

11. Jean Varloot, Introduction to *Le Rêve de D'Alembert*. The role of monsters in Diderot's work has been thoroughly discussed in a monograph by Emita B. Hill, "The role of 'le monstre' in Diderot's thought," *Studies on Voltaire and the Eighteenth Century* 97 (1972): 147-361; cf. also Hill's "Human nature and the moral monster," *Diderot Studies* 16 (1973): 91-117.

12. *Le Neveu de Rameau*. The verbal form *dissembler* seems to have been forged by Diderot in *Le Neveu de Rameau*, and its meaning is therefore subject to dispute. The Barzun translation of this sentence ("He has no greater opposite than himself") splits the character into polar opposites. While the context does provide some justification for this interpretation, one may also justifiably read the French text in terms not of contrast but of generation of difference *from oneself.*

13. *Le Rêve de D'Alembert*, 38-39.

14. Ibid., 57.

15. Ibid., 58.

16. Derrida, *De la grammatologie.*

17. Raymond Joly, *Deux etudes sur la préhistoire du réalisme* (Quebec: Laval University Press, 1969), 38.

18. *Le Rêve de d'Alembert*, 71-72.

19. Georges Bataille, "Les Larmes et les rois," *Botteghe oscure* 17 (1956): 43-44. I wish to thank Denis Hollier for having brought this article to my attention.

20. Walter Rex interprets this detail psychologially: "Suzanne's unspoken love for this Mother Superior—the culmination of all the passionate affections of the three convents,— means love of the society of women, . . . love of the cloister, and before Suzanne can get free and out of these walls, she will have to put behind her, and even kill off, her own secret desires." "Secrets from Suzanne," in *The Pull of the Opposite: Essays on Subversion, Eroticism, and Music in the French Enlightenment* (unpublished manuscript, 1982), 230. I thank Professor Rex for having allowed me to consult this manuscript.

21. *La Religieuse*, 207-8.

22. Ibid., 208.

23. Ibid., 209.

24. Ibid., 210.

25. Cf. M. Wartofsky's important article, "Diderot and the Development." For a brilliant Derridian reading of Diderot's political and sexual economy, see Elisabeth de Fontenay, "Diderot gynécome," *digraphe* 7 (1976). 29-50.

26. Whether one should speak of a "Préface-Annexe" (following Assézat) or simply of a "Preface," whether this text should be published before or after the body of the novel, these remain lively topics for critical debate. See the introductions of Herbert Dieckmann and Georges May to the Hermann edition of *La Religieuse*.

27. Cf. Hauser, *Social History of Art*; Szondi, "Denis Diderot."

Chapter 5. A Novel World (Bougainville as Supplement)

1. J.-J. Rousseau, *Oeuvres complètes* 3 (Paris: Pléiade, 1959), 213-14. Translation by Roger D. Masters and Judith R. Masters in Rousseau, *The First and Second Discourses* (New York: St. Martin's Press, 1964), 212-13.

2. H. de Romance de Mesnon, *De la lecture des romans, fragment d'un manuscrit sur la sensibilité* (Paris, 1785), 17.

3. Cf. Celati, *op. cit.*; Michèle Duchet, *Anthropologie et histoire au siècle des lumières* (Paris, Maspéro, 1971).

4. Celati, *Finzioni occidentali*, 41.

5. "'Avventura' ne linguaggio sei-settecentesco significa il capitale investito in un'impresa commerciale in terre lontane . . . [In logbooks of voyages] la prova delle cose o dell'osservazione coincide con l'ottica della scoperta: i dettagli tecnici, le singolarità empiriche, servono agli adetti ai lavori per navigazioni vere in luoghi non ancora visitati. E questo linguaggio bureaucratico la prima cosa che Robinson Crusoe impara quando diventa marinaio." Ibid., 40.

6. Louis-Antoine Bougainville, *Voyage autour du monde* (Paris: Saillant and Nyon, 1772 [1st ed., 1771]). All subsequent references are to this two-volume edition.

7. Ibid., 1, xv-xvi.

8. See chapters 1 and 2, above.

9. Bougainville, 1, xxxix.

10. Ibid., 1, xxxviii-xxxix.

11. Ibid., 1, xxxix.

12. See epigraph and note 1, this chapter.

13. Bougainville, 1, 262.

14. Ibid.

15. Ibid., 294.

16. Ibid., 264.
17. Ibid., 297-98.
18. Ibid., 299; 301-2.
19. Ibid., 300-301.
20. Ibid., 291.
21. Cf. Josephs, *Diderot's Dialogue.*
22. See above, 24.
23. The name, Pécherais, was given to these Indians by the French crew.
24. Michael Levey, *From Rococo to Revolution* (New York: Oxford University Press, 1977), 161.
25. One of these "men" (the companion of Commerson, the ship's naturalist) turned out to be a woman in disguise.
26. Roland Barthes, *Le Degré zéro de l'écriture* (Paris: Seuil, 1953).
27. Bougainville, 1, 299.

Chapter 6. Conclusions

1. An excellent work on this subject in the tradition of the Frankfurt School is William Leiss, *The Domination of Nature* (New York: Braziller, 1972).
2. Hauser, *Social History of Art*, part 5, i.
3. Cf. René Girard. *Mensonge romantique et vérité romanesque* (Paris: Grasset, 1961).
4. Cf. Carroll, "The Alterity of Discourse."
5. Bakhtin, "Formes du temps et du chronotope," 1937-38, rev. 1973; in *Esthétique et théorie du roman* (Paris: Gallimard, 1978), 235.
6. As Todorov says (*Mikhaïl Bakhtine*, chap. 6), Bakhtin was less interested in the traditional genre "novel" than in the dialogic principle that it exemplified for him.
7. Bakhtin, "Formes du temps," 237.
8. Ibid.
9. Todorov, *Mikhaïl Bakhtine*, 128.
10. Bakhtin, "Formes du temps," 389.
11. Ibid., 238, note 1.
12. Ibid., 393-94.
13. Ibid.
14. Ibid., 394.
15. Ibid.
16. Cf. Carroll, "The Alterity of Discourse," and Mehlman, *Cataract.*
17. See Samuel Weber, "Capitalizing History: Notes on the *Political Unconscious*," *Diacritics* (Summer 1983); 14-28; and Carroll, "The Alterity of Discourse."

Afterword

1. *Diderot's Selected Writings*, selected and edited, with an introduction and notes by Lester G. Crocker (London: Collier-Macmillan, 1966), 110.
2. Cf. Albert O. Hirschman, *The Passions and the Interests: Political Arguments for Capitalism before Its Triumph* (Princeton: Princeton University Press, 1977).
3. *Diderot's Selected Writings*, 111.
4. Ibid., 110.
5. The following remarks are indebted to Odo Marquard, "Kompensation: Überlegungen zu einer Verlaufsfigur geschichtlicher Prozesse," *Historische Prozesse*, edited by K.-G. Faber and Ch. Meier (Munich: dtv, 1978), and to the encyclopedia article "Kompensation" by the same author in *Historisches Wörterbuch der Philosophie*, vol. 4 (Basel: Schwabe, 1976).

6. Cf., for example, Moses Mendelssohn, *Schriften zur Philosophie, Ästhetik und Apologetik*, edited by M. Brasch (Leipzig: Brockhaus, 1880), vol. 2, 100, and the discussion between Lessing, Mendelssohn, and Nicholai in their *Briefwechsel über das Trauerspiel*, edited, with annotations and afterword, by J. Schulte-Sasse (Munich: Winkler, 1972).

7. The following summary is primarily based on Niklas Luhmann, *Gesellschaftsstruktur und Semantik*, vols. 1 and 2 (Frankfurt: Suhrkamp, 1980/81) and on his *Liebe als Passion* (Frankfurt: Suhrkamp, 1982).

8. Adam Ferguson, *An Essay on the History of Civil Society*, edited, with an introduction by Duncan Forbes (Edinburgh: University of Edinburgh Press, 1966), 19.

9. Cf. my chapters on the social history of the German drama of Enlightenment and of the aesthetics of Lessing and his contemporaries in *Hansers Sozialgeschichte der deutschen Literature*, vol. 3, edited by Rolf Grimminger (Munich: Hanser, 1980), 304-326, 423-499.

10. Immanuel Kant, *The Critique of Judgement*, translated by J. C. Meredith (Oxford: Oxford University Press, 1952), 185. I changed the translation slightly where it seemed necessary. Translating *"Lohngeschäft"* as "contract work," for example, partly loses the original term's reference to the world of business.

11. Cf. the documents that form the basis of the first four chapters in Weinstein's and Platt's *The Wish to Be Free: Society, Psyche, and Value Change* (Berkeley: University of California Press, 1969).

12. I am referring here not so much to an ongoing discussion in this country (see especially Christopher Lasch, *The Culture of Narcissism: American Life in an Age of Diminishing Expectations* [New York: Norton, 1978] and *Telos*'s special issue on narcissism [no. 44, Summer 1980]), which I find to be filled with unreflected generalities, but to medical/psychiatric publications in Europe and their application to historical issues. See especially Hans Kilian, *Das enteignete Bewußtsein: Zur dialektischen Sozialpsychologie* (Neuwied: 1971); Igor A. Caruso, *Narzissmus und Socialisation: Entwicklungspsychologische Grundlagen gesellschaftlichen Verhaltens* (Stuttgart: Klett, 1976); and the excellent application of the results of this discussion to the history of linguistics and of philosophical concepts in Hans-Jürgen Fuchs, *Entfremdung und Narzissmus: Semantische Untersuchungen zur Geschichte der "Selbstbezogenheit" als Vorgeschichte von französisch "amour-propre"* (Stuttgart: Metzler, 1977).

13. Fuchs, *Entfremdung und Narzissmus*; Luhmann, *Gesellschaftsstruktur und Semantik* and *Liebe als Passion*; Jean-Robert Armogathe, "Une secte-fantôme au dix-huitième siecle: Les egoistes." Thesis, Sorbonne, 1970.

14. Cf. Paul O. Kristeller, "The Modern System of Arts: A Study in the History of Aesthetics," *Journal of the History of Ideas* 12 (1951): 496-527, and vol. 13 (1952): 17-46.

15. Martin Fontius, "Ästhetik contra Technologie—eine Voraussetzung bürgerlicher Literaturauffassung," *Funktion der Literatur: Aspekte—Probleme—Aufgaben* (Berlin: Aufbau, 1975), 123-32; here p. 128.

16. This statement would have to be qualified for aesthetic cultures in postmodernity. See my article "Imagination and Modernity; or the Taming of the Human Mind," forthcoming in *Cultural Critique*.

17. L'Abbé Prévost, *The History of Manon Lescaut and the Chevalier des Grieux* (London: G. Routledge, 1925), 50-52.

18. About Dubos, cf. the first part of an excellent article by Kurt Wölfel, "Moralische Anstalt: Zur Dramaturgie von Gottsched bis Lessing," *Deutsche Dramentheorien*, edited by R. Grimm (Frankfurt: Athenäum, 1971), 45-122.

19. Geraint Parry, "Enlightenment Government and Its Critics in Eighteenth Century Germany," *Historical Journal* (1963): 187-88.

20. Cf. "On the interpretation of Nature," in *Diderot's Selected Works*, 74.

21. *Diderot's Selected Works*, 167.

22. Cf. the case of Lessing in Germany, which I analyzed in my chapter on the history of the German bourgeois drama, 1730-1789, in *Hansers Sozialgeschichte*, esp. 471-73.

23. *Diderot's Selected Works*, 93-94. Cf. also Diderot's *The Paradox of Acting*, translated with annotations by W. H. Pollock (London: Chatto and Windus, 1883), 5: "even with the clearest, the most precise, the most forceful of writers, words are no more, and never can be more, than symbols, indicating a thought, a feeling, or an idea; symbols which need action, gesture, intonation, expression, and a whole context of circumstance, to give them their full significance."

24. For a description of the same development from a different perspective, see Hirschman, *The Passions and the Interests*, 14-24.

25. Cf. Weinstein and Platt, *The Wish to Be Free*, 66.

26. Max Horkheimer and Theodor W. Adorno, *Dialectic of Enlightenment*, translated by John Cumming (New York: Seabury, 1972), 12.

27. Ibid., 7.

28. Ibid., 13.

Index

Index

26, 27, *Iphigénie*, 19-20, 24, 26, *Phèdre*, 26
Rameau, Jean-François: famous last words, 14; as monster, 12, 91; paradoxical figure, 3, 4
Rameau, Jean-Philippe, 26
Reader: gender of, 12-13; as philosophe, 81; role of, 11-12; social class of, 12-13; status of, 3, 49, 52-56, 62-63, 78, 81
Rhetoric: bourgeois, 13; and class, 11-12; and dialogue, 11-12; and gender, 11-12; sentimental, 24-25. *See also* Figures, rhetorical
Richardson, Samuel: *Clarissa*, 9, 51; Diderot reader of, 8-12, 90; *Pamela*, 9; rhetoric of sentimentality, 8-9
Robespierre, Maximilien de, 25
Romance de Mesnon, H. de, 76-77
Rousseau, Jean-Jacques: *Discours sur l'origine de l'inégalité*, 76-77, 82, 86; hostility toward fictions, 90; image as supplement, 43

Sacrifice: and appropriation, 77, 92; beholder's, 87, 91; Christian, 8; in David, 25; and death, 7, 8; and detachment, 75; and eroticism, 21-22; in *Le Fils naturel*, 34-37; and materialism, 7; in the novel, 63; as quotation, 20-21; in Robespierre, 25; to science, 87; of tableau's subject, 20; temporal dimension, 23, 89-90; and virtue, 25-29
Sade, D. A. F., 55
Schiller, Friedrich, 23
Science: and appropriation of nature, 79-80; as ideology, 80-88; and sentimentality, 87, 90
Sensibilité: and family, 10-12; and movement, 10-12; and tears, 10-12
Sentimentality: and bureaucracy, 78; and death, 7-8; and dialogue, 7, 87-88; and the family, 22-23; and homosexuality, 21-22, 55, 57; and incest, 22; and materialism, 7; and movement, 10-12, 77; and philos-7-8; and repetition, 17; rhetoric of, 86; sadistic and masochistic, 55; and science, 87, 90; and virtue, 8
Singularity, empirical: and abstraction, 74; and familialization, 77-78; and generic abstraction, 60-63; as novelistic value,

46, 54
Sophocles, 13, 31
Szondi, Peter: on the *drame*, 38; on Lessing's correspondence, 24; on *The London Merchant*, 21-22; mentioned, 29, on reconciliation (*Versöhnung*), 22

Tableau: and beholder, 5-6; in Bougainville, 82-88; and *coup de théâtre*, 5, 16; as dialogue, 16-18, 20; and enlightened despotism, 43-44; and family, 85, 86; and fetishism, 18-19; framing of, 23; as genetic principle, 51; and genre, 14; as ideology, 86-88; and imaginary, 5, 16, 19-21; medieval origins of, 35; as narrative, 16-18; paradoxical structure of, 89-91; politics of, 71; and quotation, 20; and reconciliation (*Versöhnung*), 22; as repetition, 16-18; sacrificial character of, 34-37; and scopic drive, 50; as structural principle, 45; subject of, 20, 23; temporal aspects of, 25-29; as tomb (*tombeau*), 25-29; uses of, 62-63, in Wright of Derby, 86-87
Tears: and bodily conflict, 51; and bourgeois drama, 10; crocodile, 88; as dialogic, 11-12; erotic, 55; and the family, 76-77; human nature of, 10-12; and identification, 47-49, 52-53, 63; as ideology, 24-25; and laughter, 47-48, 53-54, 89; and miracles, 69-71; and movement, 13; overdetermined, 75; and pathos of discovery, 77; and pleasure, 10-12; and politics, 51; as rhetorical effect, 53-59; and sacrifice, 20-25; and *sensibilité*, 10-12; and tableau, 36
Todorov, Tzvetan, 92

Verneinung (dénégation), 18-19
Vernière, Paul: on *The London Merchant*, 21-22; mentioned, 29
Virtue: as pleasure, 11-12; and sacrifice, 8, 25-29, 35-37, 89; and sentimentality, 8
Volland, Sophie: letter to (25 July 1762), 39-44; status in dialogue, 12
Voltaire, 26

Wright, Joseph (Wright of Derby): "Experiment with an Air-Pump," 86-87; and scientific affect, 90

Jay Caplan earned his masters and doctoral degrees in French literature at Yale University and, from 1970 until 1972, participated in Roland Barthes's thesis seminar at the Ecole Pratique des Hautes Etudes in Paris. He is now associate professor of French at Amherst College.

Jochen Schulte-Sasse teaches in the humanities at the University of Minnesota and is co-editor with Wlad Godzich of the series Theory and History of Literature.